# A NEW VISION FOR

## STAFF

# Development

DENNIS SPARKS
STEPHANIE HIRSH

**Association for Supervision and Curriculum Development**
Alexandria, Virginia

**National Staff Development Council**
Oxford, Ohio

national
staff development council

National Staff Development Council
P.O. Box 240 • Oxford, Ohio 45056
Telephone: 513-523-6029 • Fax: 513-523-0638

Association for Supervision and Curriculum Development
1250 N. Pitt Street • Alexandria, Virginia 22314-1453
Telephone: 1-800-933-2723 or 703-549-9110 • Fax: 703-299-8631

Gene R. Carter, *Executive Director*
Michelle Terry, *Assistant Executive Director, Program Development*
Ronald S. Brandt, *Assistant Executive Director*
Nancy Modrak, *Director of Publishing*
John O'Neil, *Acquisitions Editor*
Julie Houtz, *Managing Editor of Books*

Kathleen Larson Florio, *Copy Editor*
Deborah Whitley, *Proofreader*
Gary Bloom, *Director, Editorial, Design, and Production Services*
Karen Monaco, *Senior Designer*
Tracey A. Smith, *Production Coordinator*
Dina Murray, *Production Assistant*
Valerie Sprague, *Desktop Publisher*

Printed in the United States of America.

July 1997 member book (pc). ASCD Premium, Comprehensive, and Regular members periodically receive ASCD books as part of their membership benefits. No. FY97-8.

ASCD Stock No.: 197018     ASCD Member price: $14.95   nonmember price: $17.95

**Library of Congress Cataloging-in-Publication Data**
Sparks, Dennis.
    A new vision for staff development / Dennis Sparks and Stephanie Hirsh.
        p.   cm.
    Includes bibliographical references.
    ISBN 0-87120-283-2 : $14.95 (members), $17.95 (non-members)
    1. Teachers—In-service training—United States.
    2. Constructivism (Education)—United States.    I. Hirsh, Stephanie.
    II. Title.
    LB1731.S64   1997
    370'.711—dc21                                                97-21007
                                                                 CIP

01 00 99 98 97     5 4 3 2 1

# A New Vision for Staff Development

# 1

# A Paradigm Shift in Staff Development

Many events of the past few years bode well for the field of staff development. Reports issued by governmental bodies, business groups, and various commissions emphasize the central role staff development must play in school reform efforts. In addition, there is greater recognition today at the local, state, and national levels that sustained, high-quality staff development is essential if all students are to achieve at high levels.

At the same time, however, more people are realizing that this professional development (the terms *staff development, professional development,* and *inservice education* will be used interchangeably throughout this book) must be considerably different than that offered in the past. Soon to be gone forever, we hope, are the days when educators (usually teachers) sit relatively passively while an "expert" exposes them to new ideas or "trains" them in new practices, and the success of the effort is judged by a "happiness quotient" that measures participants' satisfaction with the experience and their off-the-cuff assessment regarding its usefulness.

Research and experience have taught us that widespread, sustained implementation of new practices in classrooms, principals' offices, and central offices requires a new form of professional development. This staff development not only must affect the knowledge, attitudes, and practices of individual teachers, administrators, and other school employees, but it also must alter the cultures and structures of the organizations in which those individuals work. While the need to help individual teachers and administrators do their jobs better is generally recognized, it is also essential that educational leaders pay attention to organizational change—if for no other reason than to bring a sense of coherence to the reform process. Many would agree with Michael Fullan, who argues that "[t]he greatest problem faced by school districts and schools is not resistance to innovation, but the fragmentation, overload, and incoherence resulting from the uncritical acceptance of too many different innovations" (1991, p. 197).

## The Need for a New Form of Staff Development

Recognizing the link between staff development and successful educational change, Ann Lieberman, Linda Darling-Hammond, and Milbrey McLaughlin are among the leading school reformers who have called for a new form of professional development. Lieberman argues for a "radical rethinking" of professional development and points out some ironic shortcomings of the traditional approach: "What everyone appears to want for students—a wide array of learning opportunities that engage students in experiencing, creating, and solving real problems, using their own experiences, and working with others—is for some reason denied to teachers when they are learners" (1995, p. 591). She notes the similarities between the ways students learn and the ways teachers learn:

> [P]eople learn best through active involvement and through thinking about and becoming articulate about what they have learned. Processes, practices, and policies built on this view of learning are at the heart of a more expanded view of teacher development that encourages teachers to involve themselves as learners—in much the same way as they wish their students would (p. 592).

Constructing a continuum of practices that encourage teachers' growth, Lieberman describes the movement from "direct teaching" (the current dominant mode of training-focused professional development), to "learning in school," to "learning out of school." "Because 'direct-teaching' currently dominates much of what the public and many districts consider staff development," Lieberman states, "it is important that teachers, administrators, and policymakers become aware of new and broader conceptions of professional development" (p. 592). She believes that "teachers must have opportunities to discuss, think about, try out, and hone new practices" by taking new roles (e.g., teacher researcher), creating new structures (e.g., problem-solving groups), working on new tasks (e.g., creating standards), and creating a culture of inquiry. "What characterizes these examples of professional learning," Lieberman writes, "is that their life span is not one or two days. Instead, they become part of the expectations for teachers' roles and form an integral part of the culture of a school" (p. 593).

Darling-Hammond and McLaughlin (1995) suggest that staff development that is linked to a reform agenda must support a learner-centered view of teaching and a career-long conception of teachers' learning:

> The success of this agenda ultimately turns on teachers' success in accomplishing the serious and difficult tasks of *learning* the skills and perspectives assumed by new visions of practice and *unlearning* the practices and beliefs about students and instruction that have dominated their professional lives to date. Yet few occasions and little support for such professional development exist in teachers' environments (p. 597).

Darling-Hammond and McLaughlin seek a form of professional development that prepares teachers "to see complex subject matter from the perspectives of diverse students" (p. 597), and they point out that understanding cannot be developed only through traditional top-down teacher-training strategies limited to teachers' acquisition of new knowledge and skills. "Professional development today also means providing occasions for teachers to reflect critically on their practice and to fashion new knowledge and beliefs about content, pedagogy, and learners" (p. 597).

Fortunately, irresistible forces currently at work in education are creating a new form of staff development. History teaches us the power of a transforming idea, an alteration in world view so profound that all that follows is changed forever. Such a paradigm shift is now rapidly transforming the discipline of staff development.

3

## Three Powerful Ideas

Three powerful ideas are currently altering the shape of schools in the United States and the staff development that occurs within them. These ideas are results-driven education, systems thinking, and constructivism.

### RESULTS-DRIVEN EDUCATION

Results-driven education judges the success of schooling not by the courses students take or the grades they receive, but by what they actually know and can do as a result of their time in school. (The term *results-driven education* is used throughout to avoid the many connotations associated with the term *outcome-based education.*) Results-driven education requires that teachers and administrators acquire new instructional knowledge and skills and alter their attitudes (e.g., from the belief that grades should be based on the bell curve to the belief that virtually all students can acquire the school's valued outcomes provided they are given sufficient time and appropriate instruction).

"Results are inevitable," someone once observed, and that truism captures the essence of results-driven education. Every form of education produces some results; results-driven education simply begins the educational process by stipulating the desired results as a means of designing curriculum and instruction in a way that makes those results more likely to occur.

What could be easier to understand than the notion that, as Stephen Covey puts it in *The Seven Habits of Highly Effective People,* if you want to accomplish something, you start with the end in mind? Yet, it is not uncommon that we begin the planning process by listing activities rather than specifying intended results. In schools, that approach historically has meant that we have focused on the classes students take rather than the knowledge, skills, and dispositions we expect students to acquire as a result of their experiences.

Results-driven education begins when school systems or schools clarify their educational purposes, and it is based on "the simple principle that decisions about curriculum and instruction should be driven by the outcomes we'd like children to display at the end of their educational experience" (O'Neil 1994, p. 6). According to Kathleen Fitzpatrick (1995),

4

four operational principles guide results-driven education: (1) clarity of focus, (2) beginning with the end in mind, (3) high expectations for all students, and (4) expanded opportunities for success in student learning.

In results-driven schools, the school community—which includes parents, students, and business and community representatives as well as teachers and administrators—asks itself, What should a high school graduate know or be able to do as a result of his or her education? These schools typically value the perspectives of various constituent groups in determining the desired outcomes. Results-driven education systematizes the numerous decisions teachers make each day about what is important for students to learn—what students will be held accountable for when they are quizzed, tested, or asked to do various assignments. Further, it makes these outcomes explicit for teachers, students, and parents alike.

Results-driven education represents a dramatic shift in thinking regarding the purpose of schools and what we expect of students; and in a logical progression, results-driven education for students requires results-driven staff development for educators. Traditionally, a "seat-time" view of K–12 education has led to a similar approach to staff development. Staff development departments have typically reported the number of hours of workshops or courses attended by employees and their satisfaction with those activities rather than noting any changes in on-the-job behavior or effects on students or the organization. It has become increasingly clear, however, that a seat-time view of staff development is incongruous with a results-driven educational system. Staff development's success will be judged not by how many teachers and administrators participate in staff development programs or how they perceive its value, but by whether it alters instructional behavior in a way that benefits students. The goal is improved performance—by students, staff, and the organization.

## Systems Thinking

The second transforming idea, systems thinking, has been described by Senge as "a discipline for seeing wholes. It is a framework for seeing interrelationships rather than things, for seeing patterns of change rather than static 'snapshots'" (1990, p. 69). Senge believes systems thinking is required because we are becoming overwhelmed by complexity, and systems thinking offers a language that can restructure how we think about various types of relationships and about how organizations change. "We are conditioned to see life as a series of events," Senge says, "and for every event, we think there is one obvious cause" (p. 21).

Rather than seeing events, systems thinkers see the interconnectedness of all things and understand that causality is circular rather than a straight line. As a result, changes in any part of the system—even relatively minor changes—will affect in complex ways the other parts and the system as a whole, sometimes favorably and other times unfavorably. Likewise, Michael Fullan points out that systems thinking is more than the "mere articulation of one element of a big system to another element. It's the recognition that elements dynamically interact" (O'Neil 1993, p. 11).

Thus, an important aspect of systems thinking is that change within the system is continuous; the system is always in a state of flux, which may or may not be evident at any given moment. To further complicate the situation, the changes that occur today in one part of the system may not become obvious for months or even years, which may lead observers to miss the link between two events.

Because educational leaders typically have not thought systemically, reform has most often been approached in a piecemeal fashion. For instance, graduation requirements may be increased, teachers may be trained in some new process, or decision making may be decentralized— with little thought given to how these changes influence other parts of the system. As a result, "improvements" in one area may produce unintended negative consequences in another part of the system (e.g., increasing graduation requirements in science without appropriate changes in assessment, curriculum, and instructional methods may increase the dropout rate).

To address this issue of disconnectedness, Senge encourages organizational leaders to identify points of high leverage in the system. "[S]mall, well-focused actions can sometimes produce significant, enduring improvements, if they're in the right place. Systems thinkers refer to this principle as 'leverage'" (p. 64). Applying the principle to education, change introduced into certain areas—assessment strategies, for example—can have a positive ripple effect elsewhere in the organization—in curriculum and instruction, for example. Unfortunately, these points of high leverage, where small changes can produce big results, are often the least obvious. Senge points out that

> [o]ur nonsystemic ways of thinking are so damaging specifically because they consistently lead us to focus on low-leverage changes: we focus on symptoms where the stress is greatest. We repair or ameliorate the symptoms. . . . [T]he leverage in most real-life systems, such as most organizations, is not obvious to most of the actors in those systems. They don't see the "structures" underlying their actions (p. 114).

Senge emphasizes the power of structure to influence human behavior. "When placed in the same system," he argues, "people, however different, tend to produce similar results. . . . We must look into the underlying structures which shape individual actions and create the conditions where types of events become likely" (pp. 42–43). He points out that because we don't understand the power of structures, we are unaware of their influence until we notice that we feel compelled to act in certain ways. Fortunately, we can alter the system structures within which we operate. That requires, however, the conceptual framework of structural or systems thinking. "Enthusiasm for creating our future is not enough" (p. 53).

Robert Fritz (1989) also emphasizes the power of structures and systems to influence behavior. He examines the recurring patterns that most people have experienced both personally and professionally when their persistent efforts seem to have no effect or, worse yet, the opposite of the ones intended. He argues that these unintended effects are the result of poorly understood, continuing structural conflicts that are dominant forces in our lives.

A structure, according to Fritz, includes the fundamental parts of something and their relationship to one another and to the whole. Everything has an underlying structure, Fritz says, and every structure has within it an inclination toward movement, a tendency to change from one state into another. Structures achieve their power in organizations through their influence on human behavior.

Fritz's view is based on two premises: energy always flows along the path of least resistance, and traditional problem-solving methods cannot rescue us from structural conflict. Because some structures are more useful than others in producing desired results, improvement requires the creation of new structures that propel us toward different outcomes. Structure, Fritz argues, determines behavior because it establishes the path of least resistance along which energy will flow.

Fritz points out that certain types of structures lead to "oscillation," a forward-and-back-again movement that produces a sense of accomplishment but no significant change (e.g., many people who eat less to lose weight find that after a while they have regained the pounds that were lost, and perhaps added a few more). Progress in these structures is always temporary.

Because structures have such a strong influence on behavior, the tension they create can be applied to improve performance, Fritz believes. A key question for him, then, is, What structures should I adopt to create the results I want to create? Because problem solving involves taking action to make something go away (the problem) and typically leads to oscillation, he prefers that individuals and organizations focus on creation—taking action to have something come into being. These structures, Fritz claims, produce a healthy tension that leads to resolution, not oscillation, which in turn increases the possibility and probability of further accomplishment.

Structural tension (which Fritz views as productive) occurs when we conceive of the results we want to create, thoroughly understand current reality, develop strategies to reach the intended results, and then take action. Specifically, Fritz advises that we conceive results (as schools do through their mission statements and goals), know what currently exists (by examining data and making certain that all perspectives are heard), and implement the plan.

Like many buzz words, *systems thinking* has come to mean different things to different people. Michael Holzman (1993) argues that when applied to education, the term means working every aspect of the school system (e.g., schools, district bureaucracies, state departments of education), working with every school in a system, and approaching reform systematically for the purpose of producing fundamental change:

> If teaching and learning are to improve for all students, we need change: fundamental change affecting every aspect of our schools and every school in our school systems, change from the statehouse to the classroom. In other words, we need *systemic* change (p. 18).

Systems thinking has two important implications for staff development. First, staff development must help install systems thinking at all levels within the organization so that school board members, superintendents and other central office administrators, principals, teachers, and students understand the nature and power of systems to shape events. Second, educational leaders must understand the limitations of staff development that is divorced from a systems perspective and appreciate the central role of staff development within systemic change efforts.

## CONSTRUCTIVISM

The third powerful educational idea is constructivism. Constructivists believe that learners create their own knowledge structures rather than merely receive them from others. In this view, knowledge is not simply transmitted from teacher to student, but instead is constructed in the mind of the learner. In *The Case for Constructivist Classrooms,* Jacqueline Grennon Brooks and Martin Brooks base their case for constructivism on a simple premise: "We construct our own understandings of the world in which we live" (1993, p. 4). In her preface to the book, Catherine Twomey Fosnot observes that constructivism is not a theory about instruction, but rather one about knowledge and learning in which the student is a "thinker, creator, and constructor" (p. viii).

Just as young people create their cognitive structures based on their interactions with the world, so, too, do adults construct reality based on "schemes"—categories, theories, ways of knowing that provide maps of the world (Clinchy 1995). According to Clinchy, learning occurs when events require some adaptive changes in these schemes. Constructivist theory, then, holds that the learning of both students and adults is promoted when there is a partial discrepancy between existing cognitive structures and the new experience.

From a constructivist perspective, it is critical that teachers model appropriate behavior, guide student activities, and provide various forms of examples rather than use common instructional practices that emphasize telling and directing. "[T]eachers must become constructivist," Barbara Talbert Jackson argues in her foreword to *The Case for Constructivist Classrooms.* "[T]hey must provide a learning environment where students search for meaning, appreciate uncertainty, and inquire responsibly" (p. v).

9

The use of excessive teacher talk and textbooks comes from a "transmittal" view of learning—information is simply passed from teachers or textbooks to learners via lectures, reading, and so on. According to this view, learners receive this information in exactly the same form in which it was sent by the teacher.

On the other hand, according to Brooks and Brooks, constructivist teachers encourage and accept student autonomy and initiative; use raw data and primary sources, along with manipulative, interactive, and physical materials; allow student responses to drive lessons, shift instructional strategies, and alter content; inquire about students' understandings of concepts before sharing their own understanding of those concepts; encourage students to engage in dialogue, both with the teacher and with one another; foster student inquiry by asking thoughtful, open-ended questions and encouraging students to formulate and ask their own questions; seek elaboration of students' initial responses; engage students in experiences that might engender contradictions to their initial hypotheses and then encourage discussion; provide time for students to construct relationships and create metaphors; and nurture students' natural curiosity. Teachers must also learn to understand students' points of view as instructional entry points—which means that teachers must be good listeners as well as talkers.

If the instructional goal is to help students become better problem posers and problem solvers, the classroom environment and adult modeling are critical to this success, according to Brooks and Brooks:

> When students work with adults who continue to view themselves as learners, who ask questions with which they themselves still grapple, who are willing and able to alter both content and practice in the pursuit of meaning, and who treat students and their endeavors as works in progress, not finished products, students are more likely to demonstrate these characteristics themselves (p. 9).

While many teachers agree with constructivist goals of active, mind-engaging learning and deeper understanding, the path to becoming a constructivist teacher is not easy, Brooks and Brooks admit. It "meanders through our own memories of school as students, our most cherished beliefs, and our private versions of truth and visions for the future" (p. 13). To counter these memories, they suggest that teachers study the research of Piaget, Vygotsky, Elkind, Dewey, and Gardner. Teachers should also consider programs that are based on a constructivist framework—whole-language, manipulative mathematics programs, hands-on science, and cooperative learning techniques. They suggest that resources be focused on teachers' professional development rather than on textbooks and workbooks, that school-based study groups focus on principles of human development, and that administrators and school board members regularly attend staff development programs on teaching and learning. Brooks and Brooks warn that without this kind of commitment of resources and energy, constructivist approaches to instruction may yield disappointing results:

> [U]nless teachers are given ample opportunities to learn in constructivist settings and construct for themselves educational visions through which they can reflect on educational practices, the instructional programs will be trivialized into "cookbook" approaches (pp. 121–122).

The implications of constructivism for staff development are thus profound and quite direct: constructivist classrooms cannot be created through transmittal forms of staff development. Staff development must model constructivist practices for teachers if those teachers are expected to be convinced of the validity of those practices and to understand them sufficiently well to make them an integrated part of their classroom repertoires. Rather than receiving "knowledge" from "experts" in training sessions, teachers and administrators will collaborate with peers, researchers, and their own students to make sense of the teaching/learning process in their own contexts. Staff development from a constructivist perspective will include activities such as action research, conversations with peers about the beliefs and assumptions that guide their instruction, and reflective practices such as journal keeping—activities that many educators may not even view as staff development.

Results-driven education, systems thinking, and constructivism are producing profound changes in how staff development is conceived and implemented. Some of the most important of these changes are described in the next section.

## Major Shifts in Staff Development

Although the following "shifts" represent a change in focus in the nature of staff development, the use of newer processes does not necessarily exclude the application of more traditional approaches. In essence, the shifts describe a change in practice in which certain processes are used more and others less. What is most critical is the match between learning processes and the goals of the staff development effort. The paradigm shifts briefly presented below are described in greater detail in subsequent chapters.

• *From individual development to individual development* **and** *organization development.* Too often we have expected dramatic changes in schools based solely on staff development programs intended to help individual teachers and administrators do their jobs more effectively. An important lesson from the past few years, however, has been that improvements in individual performance alone are insufficient to produce the results we desire.

It is now clear that success for all students depends upon both the learning of individual school employees *and* improvements in the capacity of the organization to solve problems and renew itself. While the knowledge, skills, and attitudes of individuals must continually be addressed, quality improvement expert W. Edwards Deming (1986) estimated that 94 percent of the barriers to improvement reside in the organization's structure and processes, not in the performance of individuals. For instance, asking teachers to hold higher expectations for students in a school that tracks students pits teachers against the system in which they work. As systems thinking has taught us, unless individual learning and organizational changes are addressed simultaneously and support one another, the gains made in one area may be canceled by continuing problems in the other.

• *From fragmented, piecemeal improvement efforts to staff development driven by a clear, coherent strategic plan for the school district, each school, and the departments that serve schools.* Educational experts such as Seymour Sarason (1991) and Michael Fullan (1991) have criticized schools for their fragmented approach to change. School improvement too often has been based on fad rather than a clear, compelling vision of the school system's future. This, in turn, has led to one-shot staff development workshops with no thought given to follow-up or how a technique fits in with those that were taught in previous years. At its worst, staff development asks teachers to implement poorly understood innovations with little support and assistance; and before they are able to approach mastery, the school has moved on to another area.

An orientation to outcomes and systems thinking has led to strategic planning at the district, school, and department levels. Clear, compelling mission statements and measurable objectives expressed in terms of student outcomes guide the type of staff development activities that would best serve district and school goals. In turn, district offices for staff development and curriculum see themselves as service agencies for schools. This comprehensive approach to change makes certain that all aspects of the system (e.g., assessment, curriculum, instruction, parent involvement) are working in tandem toward a manageable set of outcomes that are valued throughout the system.

• *From district-focused to school-focused approaches to staff development.* Although districtwide awareness and skill-building programs sometimes have their place, more attention today is aimed at helping schools meet their improvement goals. Schools set their goals both to help the school system achieve its long-term objectives and to address challenges unique to their students' needs.

School improvement efforts in which the entire staff seeks incremental annual improvement related to a set of common objectives (e.g., helping all students become better problem solvers, increasing the number of students who participate in a voluntary community service program to 100 percent) over a three- to five-year span are viewed as the key to significant reform. As a result, more learning activities are designed and implemented by school faculties, with the district's staff development department providing technical assistance and functioning as a service center to support the work of the schools.

• *From a focus on adult needs and satisfaction to a focus on student needs and learning outcomes, and changes in on-the-job behaviors.* Rather than basing staff development solely upon the perceptions of educators regarding what they need (e.g., to learn about classroom management), staff development planning processes are more often beginning by determining the things students need to know and be able to do and working backward to the knowledge, skills, and attitudes educators must have if those student outcomes are to be realized. This shift does not negate the value of teachers' perceptions regarding their needs, but rather places those needs within a larger context.

In addition, this shift recognizes that the ultimate criterion against which systemic change efforts must be judged is their effect on student learning. It is no longer sufficient to judge the value of staff development efforts by gathering information on participants' satisfaction with those efforts. On the other hand, it will no longer be acceptable to hold staff development solely responsible for improvement in student outcomes. Systems theory makes it clear that student outcomes are the result of complex interactions of the various parts of the system (e.g., district and school leadership, curriculum, assessment, parental involvement), and that all these parts must be critically examined to determine their influence on one another and on student learning.

• *From training conducted away from the job as the primary delivery system for staff development to multiple forms of job-embedded learning.* Critics have long argued that too much of what passes as staff development is "sit and get," in which educators are passive recipients of received wisdom. Likewise, a great deal of staff development could be thought of as "go and get" because "learning" has typically meant leaving the job to attend a workshop or other event.

Although well-designed training programs followed by coaching will continue to be the preferred method for the development of certain skills, school employees will also learn through such diverse means as action research, participation in study groups or small-group problem solving, observation of peers, journal writing, and involvement in improvement processes (e.g., participation in curriculum development and school improvement planning).

• *From an orientation toward the transmission of knowledge and skills to teachers by "experts" to the study by teachers of the teaching and learning processes.* Teachers will develop their own expertise by spending an increasingly larger portion of their work day in various processes that will help them continually improve their understanding of the teaching and learning process. Teachers will regularly use action research, study groups, and the joint planning of lessons, among other processes, to refine their instructional knowledge and skills.

• *From a focus on generic instructional skills to a combination of generic and content-specific skills.* Although staff development related to cooperative learning, mastery learning, and mastery teaching, among other topics, will continue to have its place, more staff development of various forms will focus on specific content areas such as mathematics, science, language arts, and social studies. Recent studies have revealed the importance of teachers' possessing a deeper understanding of both their academic disciplines and of specific pedagogical approaches tailored to those areas.

• *From staff developers who function primarily as trainers to those who provide consultation, planning, and facilitation services as well as training.* Staff developers are more frequently called on today to facilitate meetings or to assist various work groups (e.g., a school faculty, the superintendent's cabinet, a school improvement team) solve problems or develop long-range plans. While staff developers will continue to provide training in instructional areas, results-driven education and systems thinking have placed teachers, administrators, and school employees in new roles (e.g., team leader, strategic planning team member). Successful performance in these roles requires training in such areas as conducting effective meetings.

• *From staff development provided by one or two departments to staff development as a critical function and major responsibility performed by all administrators and teacher leaders.* Job-embedded staff development means that superintendents, assistant superintendents, curriculum supervisors, principals, and teacher leaders, among others, must see themselves as teachers of adults and view the development of others as one of their most important responsibilities. Individuals who perform these roles are increasingly being held accountable for their performance as planners and implementers of various forms of staff development.

As responsibility for staff development has been spread throughout the school system, the role of the staff development department has become even more important. Staff development departments are assisting teachers and administrators by offering training and ongoing support in acquiring the necessary knowledge and skills to assume their new responsibilities, by providing one-to-one coaching of these individuals in their new roles, and by facilitating meetings that are best led by individuals who are outside that particular group.

• *From staff development directed toward teachers as the primary recipients to continuous improvement in performance for everyone who affects student learning.* To meet the educational challenges of the 21st century, everyone who affects student learning must continually upgrade his or her skills— school board trustees, superintendents and other central office administrators, principals, teachers, the various categories of support staff (e.g., aides, secretaries, bus drivers, custodians), and parents and community members who serve on policy-making boards and planning committees.

• *From staff development as a "frill" that can be cut during difficult financial times to staff development as an indispensable process without which schools cannot hope to prepare young people for citizenship and productive employment.* Both the professional development of school employees and significant changes in the organizations in which they work are required if schools are to adequately prepare students for life in a world that is becoming increasingly complex. Fortunately, results-driven education and systems thinking provide us with the intellectual understanding and the means to create the necessary reforms.

## What Implementation Will Bring

The shifts described above are significant and powerful. They are essential to the creation of learning communities in which everyone—students, teachers, principals, and support staff—are both learners and teachers. All of the things described above will serve to unleash the most powerful source of success for all students—the daily presence of adults who are passionately committed to their own lifelong learning within organizations that are continually renewing themselves.

The following chapters describe how schools and school systems across North America are implementing these shifts. Because an organization may be implementing more than one shift simultaneously or because some staff development efforts fit into more than one category, the activities described may sometimes fit appropriately into several chapters. The final section of this book provides information that will enable readers to contact the persons who describe their work in the following chapters.

# 2

## Individual Development and Organization Development

S ystems thinking teaches us that individual learning and organizational changes must occur simultaneously and support one another if the gains made in one area are not to be eliminated by
continuing problems in another. Too often we have harbored unrealistic
hopes that dramatic changes would occur in schools as a result of staff
development programs designed to help individual teachers and administrators. These programs are built on the assumption that improved
performance will be achieved when individuals learn how to do their
jobs better. For instance, teachers attend workshops on instructional
skills such as cooperative learning that are intended to change their
practice and subsequently improve the learning of students. Principals
attend workshops on supervisory skills so they can provide more effective feedback to teachers so that they, in turn, will improve their teaching.

The flaw in this assumption is the failure to recognize that too often
organizational constraints make it difficult for individuals to consis-
tently apply over time the understandings and skills they have acquired.
Teachers may learn a new instructional skill but find that their use of it
gradually diminishes because no one else in the school is using it or
because their principals do not support the practice.

The past few years have taught us that the results we desire require more than just improvements in the performance of individual school employees. Success for all students also requires improvements in the capacity of the organization to solve problems and continuously renew itself. This means that school systems must continually examine their policies, procedures, job descriptions, communication patterns, and decision-making processes to determine whether they are coherent and support the system's mission and goals.

To illustrate, a teacher may attend a Teacher Expectation, Student Achievement (TESA) workshop and deeply desire to apply the insights and skills acquired, only to find that the school system's long history of tracking students has so negatively affected students' attitudes about themselves and learning that the new techniques have little likelihood of success. In this case, staff development has the effect of pitting teachers against the system in which they work.

While individual learning and organization development are both essential, it is important to remember that organization development ultimately depends upon the knowledge, skills, and attitudes of individuals. For instance, district leaders—whether they work in the central office or in schools—must acquire the knowledge and skills related to systems thinking. They must also be skillful in diagnosing organizational strengths and weaknesses and in designing appropriate interventions.

* * *

Organization development can take many forms in school systems. It may be the teaching of special skills to school employees who will facilitate meetings and assist in conflict resolution. It may involve the training of process observers who attend meetings to provide feedback to participants on the group's performance. It may include the use of outside consultants who diagnose and design interventions around common organizational problems, such as communication problems, interpersonal conflicts, and fragmented improvement efforts. Profiled in this chapter are two school systems—the Adams 12 Five Star Schools in Northglenn, Colorado, and the Northeast Independent School District in Texas—that are applying organization development practices to school reform.

## Adams 12 Five Star Schools

According to Joellen Killion, a staff development trainer for the Adams 12 Five Star Schools, the school system has had a long history of training in both content-specific and generic instructional skills. With the hiring of Jim Mitchell as superintendent in the early 1980s, the district quickly moved to site-based management, and a new need emerged. "We soon recognized," Killion recalls, "that we needed to do a whole new type of work in staff development if our new shared decision-making and decentralization efforts were to be successful." Mitchell left the district in 1994. Judith Margrath-Huge, his successor, has focused on improving student learning, viewing collaboration and shared decision making as means to that end.

Killion remembers that as the district became involved in designing new training programs in areas such as team building, conflict management, and consensus decision making, they became aware that they were no longer just doing skill-building for individuals, but were changing the capacity of the organization to do its work:

> In the past our programs were job specific, so we would offer something for teachers in their classrooms. As we started to do more process skills, we realized that those skills weren't necessarily job specific. When we did training we were also simultaneously putting into the field people who had the capacity to participate in the school improvement effort and to do the facilitation, no matter what their job title. We wanted to make certain that *every* employee had this capacity—bus drivers, custodians, food service workers, and secretaries. Not everyone participated in formal training, but those who didn't learned the skills by actually engaging in the processes themselves. This process helped shift our staff development emphasis from the individual to the organization.

Killion reports a growing awareness that staff development had to focus on the individual and the organization simultaneously and that more needed to be learned about systemic change. "We knew that we had to think more closely and deeply about how things were interrelated," Killion says. "We needed to better understand the primary and secondary effects of actions that were taken."

Over several years, Killion notes, the result was an increased focus on the organization as a whole. The central office was restructured into circles of influence rather than a pyramid of authority. Positions and responsibilities were realigned so that services could be provided to schools in a better manner. Policy and contractual language was revised to reflect the move away from centralized control.

Killion points out another result: the superintendent's cabinet—called the District Coordinating Team—models shared decision making and the importance of continuous learning for all employees. Representatives of all departments and units serve on the cabinet, including the presidents of the parent organization and the support staff union. In addition, rather than replace an assistant superintendent whose job had included supervision over the departments of curriculum, staff development, and school improvement, a coleadership process was initiated among the three department heads. This eliminated a layer of management and coordinated the work of the three departments. The three individuals now make decisions about their departments by consensus.

Killion recognizes the intertwining of individual and organization development. "How do we develop the capacities of individuals who are the organization so that the organization will do what we want it to do?" she asks rhetorically. She continues:

> The image that we have is that the organization is its individuals, and the individuals must exhibit the values, skills, and knowledge that we want the organization to be known for. Those two things must work simultaneously. However, we also have thought about the structure of the organization—the reporting mechanisms, policies, communication patterns, the formation of cross-departmental project teams. For instance, when the staff development department creates its budget, we call in a cadre of people who access staff development and ask them what we should be doing.

## Northeast Independent School District

The Northeast Independent School District (Northeast ISD) is one of 13 school systems in Bexar County, Texas, that serve the city of San Antonio. It is an urban/suburban district with 50,000 students in 45 schools. Director of Staff Development Linda O'Neal reports to the supervisor for curriculum and development. The department consists of the director, a part-time program director, and a secretary.

According to O'Neal, the district has spent nearly a decade focusing on instructional improvement. More recently, the district has added a focus on school and organization development to its commitment to the development of individual employees.

O'Neal reports that a districtwide steering committee creates a broad framework for using the six days of the school calendar set aside specifically for staff development. For the 1995–1996 school year the calendar included one-half day for a whole-district gathering, a day for districtwide curriculum meetings, one-half day for cluster/feeder system schools, and four days for site-based staff development. Each school submits a plan for staff development, including an evaluation component that links the effort to student achievement.

A major instructional improvement initiative has been the implementation of a program that combines models of teaching and 4-MAT, O'Neal notes. 4-MAT is a system for instructional design that integrates four learning styles and brain hemisphere research. Fourteen campuses are taking part. Each school has formed study groups and has provided for ongoing coaching.

The district began the process with principals by building their knowledge base and leadership capacity for the initiative. Next, a training-of-trainers model facilitated districtwide implementation. "The district has experienced great success with this empowerment model," O'Neal says. Five to 10 teachers provide annual updates and work with the campus improvement committees to help design and facilitate the staff development for the next year. Individual schools collect student data to determine the effectiveness of their efforts, with two of the campuses using the Concerns-Based Adoption Model to track teachers' application of the new practices.

Additional individual development support for administrators is provided by the Human Side of Change, a program developed by the International Training and Development Consortium that prepares people to function more effectively in organizations no matter what their role. The program provides participants with leadership profiles accompanied by customized coaching for each participant.

According to O'Neal, the district's commitment to school-based improvement is evident in its approach to helping schools plan effective staff development. The district provides training sessions for school committees on how to write a school improvement plan that meets district requirements. After a school drafts its initial plan, a coach meets with the committee to critique and edit the plan. The school then submits the plan to the central office, where it is evaluated by the staff development and curriculum staff, who look specifically at the student achievement data and whether the intended interventions will lead to the kinds of changes outlined in the plan. "If they are not up to district standards, the committee is invited in for additional assistance," O'Neal reports. The process ensures a consistent quality product across the district. "Qualitative measures indicate the plans are getting stronger and the clients feel more supported," she says.

In addition to its attention to individual and school-based learning, the staff development department is being used more and more to provide organizational support for a variety of district initiatives, O'Neal reports. For instance, the department assists the superintendent and school board president in the superintendent's evaluation process, which includes the writing of annual action plans. "Another exciting initiative is the new process for hiring campus administrators," O'Neal says. "Focus groups are used to solicit input from parents, teachers, and others to identify the leadership characteristics of the administrator they want to hire."

According to O'Neal, at the superintendent's request, principals' meetings have also changed in the Northeast ISD to include a dialogue process before the regular business meeting. In addition, all the district's principals have been trained in the Dupont Leadership Process to enhance their management skills for committee meetings related to campus improvement. Additionally study teams of administrators and consultants have been formed to explore leadership issues as well as new ways to boost student achievement.

In the summer of 1995 the district held a technology summit planned and conducted by the staff development department. The desired result was a district vision for technology and an outline of the components necessary to achieve the vision. To demonstrate the level of success of the summit, a bond proposal was subsequently approved by voters.

The department is working hard to change the district's belief system regarding staff development. "There are still those who believe if it's not a workshop it is not staff development," O'Neal says. But such views don't deter the department, as she makes clear:

> Our commitment to student success and the intensity of our work keep us busy. We continue to learn from other districts who are as committed and focused on staff development that leads to individual and organizational improvements for children.

# 3

---

# A Clear, Coherent Plan

chools have long been criticized for their fragmented approach to change. Too often, critics charge, school improvement has been based on fad rather than a clear vision of the school system's future. This, in turn, has led to one-shot staff development workshops of the "dog-and-pony-show" variety, with little consideration of how the program will continue or how this particular event fits in with earlier efforts. At its worst, this form of staff development asks teachers and administrators to implement poorly understood innovations with little support. Before they are able to master the new technique or skill, the school has moved on to other topics.

In recent years, an orientation to outcomes and to systems thinking has led to the use of strategic planning at the district, school, and department levels. These plans are typically developed by a broad-based team that includes teachers, administrators, classified and support staff, school board members, parents, community members, and older students. A clear, compelling mission statement and measurable objectives make up the core of the plan. The mission and objectives, in turn, guide staff development activities that will best serve district and school goals.

As a result of this approach, district offices for staff development and curriculum become service agencies for schools. Staff development becomes a means to an end rather than the end in itself; it helps educators close the gap between current practices and the practices needed to achieve the desired outcomes. This comprehensive approach to change assures that all aspects of the system—for example, policy, assessment, curriculum, instruction, parent involvement—are working together with staff development toward the achievement of a manageable set of student outcomes that the entire system values. The following examples show how school districts in Connecticut, Nebraska, and Colorado have sought improvement through comprehensive planning with staff development as a core component.

## Pomperaug Regional School District #15

The 280 teachers in the Pomperaug Regional School District #15 in Middlebury, Connecticut, serve 3,500 students in six schools. According to Assistant Superintendent Michael Hibbard, staff development in the district has been driven since the late 1980s by a K–12 performance-based learning and assessment program. Rather than being guided by a strategic plan, the Region 15 vision was crafted incrementally by teachers and administrators who learned during each step in the process what the next step would be.

The impetus for change came in 1987 when problems with the district's traditional curriculum review process became obvious. "We had become aware that we had to focus on student performance rather than on inputs or activities. Consequently, we asked teachers what we should do differently with the whole process of creating curricula and planning instruction and assessment," Hibbard recalls. His account describes an important shift in thinking that occurred:

> Through districtwide K–12 conversations regarding language arts, we tried to identify what we wanted kids to be like when they left us and then to back down through the curriculum to come to some agreement about what really were outcomes of importance. That conversation revealed to us that we were beginning to view students not as absorbers of information that we gave them, but as producers, as constructors. Without intending it, we had begun to accept the tenets of cognitive theory.

From that beginning, Region 15 started to shape all curriculum based on "big ideas and essential questions" culled from national standards, such as those provided by the American Association for the Advancement of Science. The next step, according to Hibbard, was to embed performance tasks in the curriculum rather than adding them on at the end. These tasks, then, not only provided assessment information for teachers and others, but were good learning experiences for students as well. Teachers learned to create detailed lists of what they expected students to learn in terms of content, process skills, and work habits. These lists, in turn, gave students a way to focus on self-assessment of their knowledge and skills and provided teachers with a means to communicate more effectively with one another and with parents. Hibbard points out that as the district went through this process in the various subject areas, it "began to articulate the best practices that were emerging, which in turn help to continue to shape the vision."

According to Hibbard, the school system understands that it will take at least five years to change the culture of a school and even longer to change the culture of the district. That change requires a sustained focus on improving student performance and the synergy that comes from simultaneous top-down and bottom-up collaboration.

Hibbard uses the terms *scout, pioneer,* and *settlers* to describe phases in the change process:

> Scouts begin the work when the outcomes are very uncertain and the strategies to obtain them are even less defined. Scouts find the path and invent strategies to follow it. Pioneers take what the scouts have created and make them more "user friendly" as they clarify the targets and modify the strategies. Scouts are the mentors of the pioneers. The work of the scouts and pioneers takes two to five years. They then engage the settlers in learning to use the new strategies.

Teachers in the district, Hibbard says, go through several stages of professional growth as they learn new ways of teaching: orientation, mechanical use, refinement, integration, and innovation. At the orientation level, teachers get their "feet on the ground." At the level of mechanical use, teachers "go by the book." During the phases of refinement, integration, and innovation, teachers adapt the strategies to learners' needs, make new connections between strategies and learning outcomes, and create new strategies that improve student performance even further. "An educator at the integration or innovation levels needs a much different environment of support than one at the orientation or mechanical levels," he points out.

According to Hibbard, in addition to training in areas such as cooperative learning, the school district encourages professional growth through cognitive coaching and through the development of teacher and administrator portfolios. The portfolios are intended to show how administrators make decisions that affect the performance of teachers and how teachers make decisions that affect student performance, Hibbard says. He elaborates:

> The teacher shows how he or she makes decisions to create and use instruction and assessment to improve student performance over the long run. The administrator shows how he or she makes decisions to provide leadership and management skills to help teachers make decisions to improve student performance according to the priorities of the school and school district.

The ultimate beneficiary of all this effort has been students, Hibbard contends. "Both internal and external sources of data show strong improvements in student performance."

## Westside Community Schools

The Westside, Nebraska, Community Schools began 50 years ago as a suburban school district. Today, as a result of Omaha's growth, the district is surrounded by the city. The Westside Community Schools serve 4,800 students at a high school, a middle school, and 10 elementary schools. Although 80 percent of the community no longer has children enrolled in the school system, taxpayers continue to be supportive of the schools, according to Director of Staff Development Jacquie Estee. "The district is known nationwide for its history of excellence, commitment to innovation, and willingness to put resources where they are needed."

Estee describes the Westside Community School District as a pioneer in strategic planning. Since the early 1980s the district has been guided by a series of five-year plans. Every two years a strategic planning committee, using a systematic planning method and led by a trained planning facilitator, analyzes data, reviews the status of the previous plan, and modifies the plan to address current needs. The district's plan is converted to specific programs through the action planning process, in which teams are formed to develop plans for implementing each objective and strategy. With the creation of the first strategic plan in 1983, the district established a staff development framework. Estee describes the plan's effect:

> We had always been a district that provided teachers with multiple opportunities to grow. But the strategic plan required we build a framework and foundation to ensure greater success as a result of our investments in staff development. We went from being a district that provided inservice opportunities to a district that for the first time put its resources and support behind a comprehensive staff development program.

Staff development in the district is defined as an ongoing, job-related program designed to enhance, maintain, and refine competencies for all staff, Estee says. It is guided by the beliefs that staff development is an essential component of school improvement and that its ultimate goal is increased student success.

Six objectives and six strategies guide the district's current strategic plan. According to Estee, although staff development is key to the achievement of all objectives and strategies, staff development is most critical to the district's "quality improvement" strategy, which states: "We will develop and implement a plan for the district and each school to have an ongoing process for quality improvement that is client-oriented and data driven."

The staff development plan takes its lead from the district plan, Estee notes. Current objectives address teacher competency in the coordination of curriculum, instruction, and assessment, and proficiency in the use of technology. Another objective addresses administrators' and supervisors' roles in implementing staff development at school sites. "The plan has given the community a way of thinking about staff development and enhanced their understanding of the need for resources to support it," she says. Within the context of the plan, expectations are established for district, school, and individual levels of participation. District-level staff development addresses priority needs of the district strategic plan and curriculum adoptions. A school committee determines building-level staff development based on a school improvement plan; personal growth plans guide individual choices.

The district has guidelines for the building-level staff development plans, Estee says. "The district recognizes that change does not result from one-shot workshops and that substantive change requires high-quality, ongoing staff development with support and follow-up in the classroom." Each plan must include a vision statement, needs assessment, goals, a training plan, follow-up activities, a midyear progress check, an evaluation component, and an end-of-year feedback process. Building-based cadre members, trained through the staff development department, help schools design and implement their plans. Supplementary funding from the district helps schools achieve their goals.

Although the staff development department consists of only a full-time director and a secretary, staff members from throughout the system may be recruited to help the department achieve its goals. Through the creation of part-time positions or the use of released time, these individuals can help schools with the implementation of school improvement plans, instructional training, or other areas where special staff expertise may be required. "The district invests in the development of facilitation skills and a minimum of one key area of content expertise for each of these individuals," Estee explains. For example, current district priorities include the implementation of new science and math curriculums; as a result, full-time specialists were hired for two years to facilitate the process. "This means every teacher will be visited and follow-up support provided to ensure districtwide implementation of the new curriculum," Estee says.

Another way in which the districts taps the skills of its staff members is the Technology Team. This group of individuals, highly knowledgeable in the use of all forms of technology, assist staff in technology planning and implementation.

Estee concludes with this overview of staff development in Westside Community Schools:

> Everyone in our school system is viewed as a staff developer. The department continuously pulls together different groups of people to assist with the development of various programs. As a result, staff members know about quality staff development and what to expect from the department.

## Aurora Public Schools

In the Aurora Public Schools, a district in suburban Denver, Colorado, with more than 27,000 students, staff development is driven by both district and school strategic plans. In 1989 the district made a commitment to strategic planning as a way to increase decentralization and community involvement. In addition, the district uses shared decision making, performance-based education, and performance-based graduation requirements in its quest to develop lifelong learners who are successful not only in school, but also in life.

According to Kay Shaw, director of the district's staff development program, the result of the first year of strategic planning was a district mission statement and 28 goals for student learning. In its effort to increase ownership of and commitment to the process and goals, the Strategic Planning Committee established procedures that ensured that all recommendations were reviewed by the Aurora staff and stakeholders. As a result of this involvement, in the second year of the plan the 28 goals were clustered around five learner outcomes: self-directed learner, collaborative worker, complex thinker, community contributor, and quality producer. In addition, content standards were developed in eight areas to include the basic knowledge and skills for each subject and the complex thinking processes necessary for students to apply these basics successfully throughout life. Students qualify for graduation by demonstrating their knowledge and skills in the content areas.

"People immediately questioned our intentions—What do you mean we haven't been teaching complex thinking?" Shaw remembers. This concern and others led the district leadership to find ways to validate the work that had preceded strategic planning and to infuse that work into the new performance-based program. The staff development department then facilitated a brainstorming process at each site to discuss what the site was currently doing to address the five learner outcomes and elicit suggestions of what more could be done. This provided a departure point for further action planning.

To establish readiness for the action planning, the district entered a design phase, Shaw recalls. To demonstrate its commitment to "stop the old and start with the new" the district halted all curriculum writing during the 1991–1992 school year. Because Aurora Public Schools is known nationally for its high-quality curriculum, this decision demonstrated clearly the district's commitment to the strategic plan. "It showed people that the district was serious about stopping things to do more important things, and not implementing everything on top of what we were already doing," Shaw says. In place of curriculum writing, staff and parents identified eight content areas, and then a process for establishing proficiencies and benchmarks was initiated.

Money previously used for curriculum development provided resources to design and deliver awareness workshops on seven priority areas identified in the strategic plan, including change, classrooms of the future, multicultural education, and alternative assessment. "We realized change was occurring in our student population, and our staff was having trouble trying to change because many of them still longed for the students and society we used to have," Shaw says. "The workshops were offered to validate that change is a normal part of life. We wanted people to know that the frustration and anxiety that accompanies it are normal but can influence our ability to accomplish our goals."

Another key facet of the design phase involved formal presentations by all schools and departments within the district regarding their visions and current programming and services. These presentations were made to small, representative, districtwide groups that listened for areas of commonality and uniqueness across the 41 schools and then made suggestions for realigning resources and developing action plans.

Four curriculum coordinators facilitated the curriculum development process. Because the issue of teaching complex thinking was particularly challenging to the staff, after a period of study the district adopted Dimensions of Learning to decrease the fragmentation of the curriculum and ensure a common focus on thinking. Dimensions of Learning is a research and theory-based framework to help teachers plan instruction to address all the critical aspects of learning.

According to Shaw, nearly all student courses and staff development courses in Aurora are now aligned with the content standards and the five learner outcomes. "Courses like raft trips, weight loss, and retirement planning are regularly turned down because they are not aligned with the district mission and goals," Shaw says. "If the course doesn't support our mission, content standards, and learner outcomes, then district resources should not be allocated to support it. However, that shouldn't stop them from doing it on their own time." All staff development courses offered for credit must answer several questions: Why do this? What are the content standards and/or learner outcomes this activity supports? How does it address complex thinking processes? How will the outcomes be measured? A review process ensures the quality of courses, Shaw notes. In addition, all staff development providers are required to participate in a presentation skills training course offered by the district.

School-based staff development in Aurora follows the same procedures, Shaw reports. Because school plans and district goals are aligned, few school-based proposals are rejected. School-based staff development is often delivered by a district staff developer, curriculum coordinator, or strategic planning facilitator in concert with local teachers. The district views school-based staff development as key to the change process. "At the school level, everyone is working extremely hard to model the five learner outcomes and improve learning opportunities for all students," Shaw says.

The implications of all this for staff development have been profound, Shaw reports. The mission of the staff development department is to serve as a resource and to facilitate implementation of the district's mission through organizational and professional development services. As individuals, schools, and other groups within the system identify their needs related to achievement of the district mission, the staff development department assists by providing organizational development/culture-building support; serving as the resource for administrators and schools in implementing shared decision making, performance-based education, and the district's content standards and learner outcomes; supporting the definition and development of mission-related competencies at both the organizational and individual level; and teaching organizational leaders to manage change. In addition the department provides consistent, integrated, and mission-related development opportunities so that staff members can help students achieve district competencies; coordinates classes and procedures for licensure; collaborates to provide training that models adult learning theory; and serves as resource and clearinghouse for information on issues related to staff development.

Shaw provides a concise summary:

> The staff development department provides the resources, support, and leadership to help assure every employee, both certificated and classified, accepts the responsibility to fulfill the district mission of developing lifelong learners who value themselves, contribute to their community, and succeed in a changing world.

# 4

# School-Focused Approaches

Educational reformers argue that reform efforts must be more school centered. This emphasis, however, meets a barrier in districts where staff development is district driven. Curriculum coordinators in these districts, for instance, update all elementary teachers on new materials, and district staff developers provide training in generic instructional techniques such as cooperative learning. Although such districtwide awareness and skill-building programs have their place within a comprehensive staff development program, more attention today is being directed at helping schools meet their specific goals for improved student learning.

In a "best of all possible worlds" scenario, each school system would have an ambitious strategic plan that provides common direction for the district as a whole. Each school, then, would develop its own long-range plan that addresses both its contributions to the district's plan and the challenges that may be unique to that school. In turn, the staff development department would develop a plan that describes how it would assist both the district and the schools in reaching their goals. The staff development department might decide, for example, to provide technical assistance to schools in the form of facilitators for meetings and offer workshops for school improvement teams on topics such as disaggregating data, understanding the change process, and managing conflict. The district might also provide districtwide training-of-trainer programs on topics such as cooperative learning that are included in the plans of a number of schools.

As this shift in focus gains momentum, more staff development is being designed and implemented by school faculties. In addition, school improvement teams are sponsoring more nontraditional forms of staff development, such as action research and study groups. The Montgomery County Schools in Maryland and the Richardson Independent School District in Texas are two examples of districts that have invested heavily in such an approach.

## Montgomery County

According to Katheryn Gemberling, deputy superintendent for instruction in the Montgomery County Schools in Maryland, a blue-ribbon committee was organized in 1987 to suggest ways the district could do a better job of attracting and retaining excellent teachers. One of the committee's 22 recommendations was the need to refocus staff development at the school level. As a result, the School Improvement Training Unit was born in 1992. Its work is complemented by the Systemwide Training Unit. "If the topic is required by the state (such as sexual harassment), is a district priority (such as multicultural education or technology education), or includes all employee groups," Gemberling says, "the Systemwide Training Unit assembles materials to assist all staff members in meeting the requirement, while the schools call on the School Improvement Training Unit to help them figure out how to adapt the information to their individual site."

The 10 members of the School Improvement Training Unit are involved in every system initiative, Gemberling notes, because it is the unit's role to make the link between system priorities—such as technology, interdisciplinary instruction, multicultural education, and performance assessment—and school-focused planning and implementation. Unit members serve on district design teams to develop and deliver the generic training, while simultaneously keeping in mind ways the program can be adapted for various schools throughout the district. School Improvement Training Unit members also serve as consultants to school staff development teams.

The district provides each Montgomery County school with a staff development budget of $2,400 to $8,000 depending on school size, according to Kathryn Blumsack, coordinator of the School Improvement Training Unit. The funds pay for substitutes, conferences, stipends, and other traditional staff development activities that are directly related to the priorities and needs described in each school's management plan. Schools use the School Improvement Training Unit to help with planning, identifying external resources, designing effective staff development efforts, adapting and managing mandates, facilitating meetings, and providing workshops on specific topics.

To better anticipate school needs and to cluster schools with similar interests, the unit reviews all school improvement plans. For instance, because interdisciplinary instruction has been a high priority at the middle-school level over the last two years, the unit has organized a week-long summer institute on this topic open to all schools. At other times, the unit "may pull together a focus group to help clarify a need or issue emerging from a single school improvement plan or several school plans to ensure the service will be on target," Blumsack says.

To help meet school needs, the district broadcasts on cable television a monthly "Teacher to Teacher" show that focuses on what Blumsack calls "hot topics." The unit trains building facilitators to use the show as one aspect of a three-hour workshop that is adapted for each school. Because the shows are cablecast, schools can tape them off air for future use.

The School Improvement Training Unit includes a dissemination specialist whose job it is to look for exemplary programs in and outside the school system and create special events for schools to learn about these programs. "We believe it is the service that keeps our schools on the cutting edge," Blumsack says, "because we are not solely focused on identified needs but paying attention to the trends in the field as well."

In July 1995 the district sent an evaluation survey to its 180 schools. Sixty-four percent of the responding schools rated the staff development planning services provided by the unit as very useful, and 33 percent rated them as somewhat useful. Seventy-five percent said the unit's training sessions were very useful, and 23 percent rated them as somewhat useful. Sixty percent of the responding schools indicated that the training resources, packets, videotapes, and articles provided by the unit were very useful; 36 percent said they were somewhat useful. Data regarding the types of services requested by schools indicate that requests for assistance have increased about 25 percent each year.

This high level of demand leads Blumsack to acknowledge one of the most frustrating aspects of the unit's work—a lack of staff to adequately serve 180 schools. Another source of frustration is the changing composition of school teams. "Team compositions change so frequently that you always seem to have teams in the beginning state," Blumsack laments. "We rarely get the opportunity to work with high-performing teams who have been together for a number of years."

The School Improvement Training Unit deals with these challenges by staying focused on its mission and its role in serving schools. "When you have a talented staff and lots of choices," she says, "it's easy to be sidetracked." To help counter that tendency, the unit often takes time to debrief its work in what are called "lessons learned" meetings.

According to Deputy Superintendent Gemberling, the most important consequence of the School Improvement Training Unit's existence is the schools' feeling of ownership over their improvement plans. "We would never go back to an exclusively top-down training model," Gemberling concludes. "The schools wouldn't let us now that they are accustomed to the funds and the flexibility."

## Richardson Independent School District

The Richardson Independent School District (RISD) is a suburban/urban school system covering portions of the cities of Dallas, Richardson, and Garland, Texas. Its 50 campuses serve 33,000 students, one-third of whom are minority. A new superintendent in 1994 and a new vision for the school system led the board of education to adopt five goals for the district and three goals that are campus-focused. The five district goals address setting world-class academic and behavioral standards, achieving those standards, retaining the best-qualified and best-trained staff for all positions, providing for all operations in a cost-effective and efficient manner, and having customers who express a high degree of satisfaction. ("Customers" in the RISD lexicon are parents.) The three building goals focus on customer satisfaction, world-class standards, and providing a good working and learning environment.

According to Jody Westbrook, formerly the district's coordinating director for staff development and now an independent consultant, the staff development department aligns its efforts with both district and school goals. Several system-level committees make decisions regarding systemwide staff development. A district education council, which is mandated by the Texas Education Agency to oversee the implementation of site-based decision making and serves in an advisory capacity to a district's board of trustees, identifies issues and needs and recommends staff development strategies. An advisory committee of teachers assists in the design of districtwide teacher induction. An administrative advisory team assists with the design and implementation of administrator training. In addition, design teams are often convened to contribute to the development of a special project or to address a crisis.

"Centrally, we plan ways to help schools go through the school improvement process," Westbrook explains. "Curriculum issues are also addressed initially at the central office." The curriculum department still offers traditional curriculum inservice sessions, but not everyone is required to attend and a variety of options are available. "Traditional curriculum training has become more customized for some groups," Westbrook says. "There are times that curriculum specialists on each campus provide staff development, as opposed to a systemwide meeting."

All systemwide training is based on an expectation that training will consist of theory, modeling, and application, Westbrook points out. Follow-up is expected to be built into everything offered by the district. "Quality tools are infused in everything we do, yet we haven't announced we are becoming a total quality school district. We are asking people to look at things in new ways," she says.

Four years ago the district made a significant shift to site-based staff development. Westbrook explains the thinking at the time:

> It appeared all the models we'd adopted called for collaboration, and yet there was no time to collaborate at the school. We studied Carl Glickman's work, which told us that improving schools have control over their staff development. We studied Fred Wood's work, which told us that school improvement doesn't occur unless staff development focuses on improving student achievement campus by campus.

At the same time, Westbrook notes, the RISD leadership recognized that the knowledge base in schools to support school-based staff development did not exist. As a result, the districtwide Professional Growth Advisory Committee recommended the schools' appointment of a Specialist-on-Site (S.O.S.). The district provided training to the specialists in the RPTIM stages of staff development (readiness, planning, training, implementation, and maintenance), Dennis Sparks and Susan Loucks-Horsley's five models of staff development (1989), Tom Guskey's (1990) model of integrating innovations, and methods of evaluating campus-based staff development.

Many of the participants in S.O.S. were recruited from another school-based staff development support mechanism, the RISD Teacher Cadre, which had been providing system and school-based staff development for more than eight years. Members of the cadre were skilled presenters who had knowledge and skills in the design of effective staff development, presentation skills, and specialized content-area knowledge. While principals were selecting their specialists, they were encouraged to consider members of the RISD Teacher Cadre working on their campuses. Although many principals selected members of the cadre, others appointed their local school council facilitator, who had received specialized training in school improvement planning and meeting facilitation.

Members of the S.O.S. corps are given clear role expectations as well as additional support and training. They are to work with their local school councils and to assist leaders of their school improvement action teams. "They are trained," Westbrook says, "to identify critical questions to pose to school improvement action teams, such as, Is what you are planning congruent with your school improvement goals? Does the plan include an appropriate model of staff development? Is there recognition of the change process and stages of concern that staff members may move through? Is the plan integrated according to Guskey's model? Does it provide for coaching? Is there an evaluation component?"

According to Westbrook, the district mandates that every school complete an annual improvement cycle that includes analyzing their data, establishing building goals focusing on student achievement, writing action plans, evaluating action plans, and adjusting their plans as necessary. Since the arrival of the new superintendent in 1994, each school has been required to adopt the three campus goals and any other they deem appropriate for that campus. Each year campuses have time to provide for the staff development they need to achieve their goals. Each campus also has a line item in its budget for staff development. The principal and staff evaluate the effectiveness of the staff development in terms of the school's success in achieving its improvement goals.

The staff development department monitors the school improvement plans from each school, Westbrook notes. It looks for trends and issues across campuses and clusters schools that have similar needs and staff development plans. The department views itself as a facilitator of the learning of all adults in the school. "When all the adults are learning and growing we believe that there is a greater likelihood that students will also be learning and growing," Westbrook concludes. "We believe that when each adult sees himself or herself as the number-one learner in that environment, we will achieve what we should achieve through staff development."

# 5

---

# Student Needs and Learning Outcomes

I n the past the content of staff development programs was often determined by a paper-and-pencil needs assessment. Teachers were asked—typically in a faculty meeting at the end of a demanding work day—to indicate or rank topics (e.g., classroom management, motivating students, teaching higher-order thinking) that they wanted to see addressed in staff development programs. Occasionally these assessments were conducted through interviews or through interactive small-group processes in which teachers would clarify their professional needs.

Critics of these processes argued that these adult-focused processes too often neglected the needs of students. "Who is speaking for the students?" they would ask. Other objections were more pragmatic: staff development programs would be designed in response to the identified needs but would too often be poorly attended (if the program was voluntary) or as negatively received by teachers as those programs that were created based on administrators' perceptions of teachers' needs. A related problem was that staff developers were often uncertain how to interpret the information provided by paper-and-pencil assessments. Did an expressed need for workshops on "classroom management" mean that the respondent was generally concerned about classroom management, or did he or she have a problem with particular types of students? Or was the concern a reflection of the need for an improved schoolwide discipline policy? Without knowing the answers to those questions staff development planners ran the risk of designing programs that entirely missed at least some of the teachers' concerns.

In the past few years, as a result of the movement to results-driven education and school-focused staff development, planning processes more often begin by determining the things students need to know and be able to do and then working backward to the knowledge, skills, and attitudes required of educators if those student outcomes are to be realized. Staff development then focuses on the gap between the required knowledge, skills, and attitudes and those currently possessed by staff members.

This shift does not negate the value of teachers' perceptions regarding their needs, nor does it suggest that teachers should not be surveyed regarding their perceptions. Rather, it places teachers' needs within a larger context that includes district and school mission and goals, student performance data, and community perceptions.

Ultimately, systemic change efforts must be judged by their contribution to student learning. It is no longer sufficient to determine the value of staff development efforts by assessing participants' perceived satisfaction with those efforts. While participants' satisfaction is a desirable goal, assessment efforts must also provide information about changes in on-the-job behavior, organizational changes, and the improved learning of all students.

At the same time it is not reasonable for staff development to be held *solely* responsible for improvement in student outcomes when factors such as district and school leadership, the application of academic standards, and the quality of the curriculum and assessment process are also critical to improving achievement. Systems theory makes it clear that student learning is the result of complex interactions among the various parts of the system (some of which the school has little or no influence over), and that all these parts must be critically examined to determine their influence on one another and on student learning. The Lawrence Public Schools in Kansas, the Adlai Stevenson High School District in Illinois, the Jefferson County Public Schools in Kentucky, and the Teachers Academy for Mathematics and Science in Chicago provide examples of an approach to staff development that focuses on student needs and learning outcomes.

## Lawrence Public Schools

The Lawrence Public Schools is a growing urban school system located between Topeka and Kansas City. It serves 10,000 students, 18 percent of whom are minority, with 25 percent receiving free or reduced lunches. The Kansas Legislature and State Board of Education view staff development as a priority and provide financial support through state legislation.

During the past 10 years the district has taken a variety of approaches to professional development. Sandee Crowther, division director for evaluation and standards, recalls that historically, staff development was planned mainly at the district level with each individual teacher or administrator choosing how to earn "inservice points" for recertification. Individuals could accumulate points through opportunities either inside or outside the district.

Recognizing that individual growth did not necessarily result in improved student learning, the district worked with a variety of consultants, including Larry Lezotte, Carl Glickman, and Bruce Joyce, to address whole-school change. A redesign of staff development in 1993 resulted in a requirement that each school develop an improvement plan to address the needs at that building. "In retrospect, the original SIP plans were somewhat superficial and not student-focused," Crowther says. She goes on to describe the state's role:

> It took a state mandate in 1992 to get school systems to take a hard look at what was happening in classrooms and demand higher levels of performance from staff and students. Consistent with the new statewide emphasis on performance-based learning and evaluation for students, the Lawrence district reorganized staff development to address performance-based learning for adults. It [was] probably the district's ongoing commitment to staff development that led to its recognition as a leader in the implementation of the state-mandated initiative referred to as Quality Performance Assessment.

Kansas has been recognized by the United States Department of Education for its framework that asks individual schools to identify learning outcomes for students and to evaluate schools according to those outcomes. "Schools are expected to use multiple measures and to triangulate their data to see if they are achieving the results they desire," Crowther explains. "Using multiple measures and analyzing student data are powerful and appropriate for encouraging high levels of student learning." The Lawrence Public Schools realigned its programs and services to ensure that students demonstrate high levels of proficiency.

According to Crowther, three processes are used to ensure student success. First, school improvement councils review the school profiles that provide information on a number of areas related to student success, including writing, science achievement, reading comprehension, and the ability to work independently. This process includes examining the current state of their schools' performance in relation to state and district standards for student outcomes. The school councils disaggregate the data and analyze it thoroughly.

During the second process the school develops an improvement plan that delineates goals for student performance in areas that need improvement. These goals must be aligned with district and state performance standards. The first part of each school improvement plan discusses the discrepancies between the state and district expectations and current levels of student performance. The plan includes a description of problems, strategies to achieve the school's goals, and three measures for demonstrating the goals are being reached. These measures most often include norm-referenced tests, state performance assessments, and district performance assessments. "What is unique is the expectation that the school will stay with an intervention and provide for continuous monitoring for a minimum of three years," Crowther notes. Once the school has selected interventions, it must describe its implementation plans as well as the evidence it will accept that changes in educators' on-the-job performance have occurred. Schools have the option of applying to the District Improvement Team for additional resources to assist in the implementation phase of the plan.

The third process, Crowther recalls, emerged from the district's adoption of a results-oriented staff development plan. For instance, all training initiatives, whether at the district or building levels, must use a design that includes presentation of theory and research, modeling, low-risk practice in the workshop setting, and on-the-job coaching to promote transfer to the workplace. The district monitors the staff development component of each school plan to ensure the approach is results-based and measured in terms of changes in job performance. "The district recognizes that without collective improvement in individual performance, changes will not occur in student performance," Crowther concludes.

## Adlai Stevenson High School District

The Adlai Stevenson High School District is a single-school district in Lincolnshire, Illinois, a suburb approximately 30 miles northwest of Chicago. The district's boundaries include all or part of 17 communities, and it accepts students from six autonomous elementary school districts. Adlai Stevenson High School enrolls 2,800 middle- to upper-middle-class students in grades 9 through 12.

The school is the only public high school in Illinois to receive an Excellence in Education recognition on two separate occasions from the U.S. Department of Education. In addition, *Redbook Magazine* has twice cited the school as one of America's Best High Schools. The school has also received commendation from the College Board Advanced Placement Program and the National Center for Effective Schools.

Ten years ago both the structure and culture of Adlai Stevenson High School reflected a philosophy of education that tracked and sorted students. As a new principal in the district, who was later promoted to the district's superintendency, Rick DuFour began his tenure by asking the community and staff to reach consensus on a new vision for the high school. A key focus of the Stevenson vision was a challenging, common core curriculum for all students. A process was then initiated to establish indicators that would provide evidence that the school was making progress toward that vision. "To borrow a phrase from Stephen Covey, we began with the end in mind," DuFour says.

The largest gap between the vision for student learning and actual practice was in the area of curriculum, DuFour recalls. Although the vision called for a core curriculum, the data gathered showed that the curriculum was either teacher or textbook driven. The vision called for students to advance to higher levels of learning by demonstrating proficiency on expected outcomes. It also required continuous monitoring of individual performance to ensure students were provided with the support they needed to succeed. "Instead we found we were a fairly traditional system in which teachers would teach what they viewed as important and award grades according to their standards or those offered by textbooks," DuFour says.

44

A three-year development process was mapped to ensure staff had the opportunity to develop the skills and knowledge they needed to make the program improvements required by the new vision. Activities during the first year focused on building a knowledge base with the staff regarding the important trends and issues in their curriculum areas. "Math teachers read articles, heard speakers, attended meetings, and studied frameworks in other systems because we didn't have the benefit of national standards at that time," DuFour recalls. In the second year of the process, each department identified the essential goals for students. The second half of that year was devoted to identifying the key outcomes for each course. "Our focus was not to create 75 behavioral objectives, but rather to identify the six or seven essential concepts each semester they wanted students to understand in a deep, rich way," DuFour says. The third year of the process was spent reaching agreement on the assessments that would be used to measure whether students achieved the outcomes.

The staff development involved in this three-year effort was concentrated and focused on related topics, such as the construction of good tests. "As a result, there were several staff development programs we didn't pursue because we stayed focused on our effort," DuFour recalls. "We don't apologize for that because we think one of the mistakes many schools make is a potpourri approach to staff development as opposed to a schoolwide, focused approach."

As principal, DuFour had to help people understand the vision, to address staff concerns, and to ensure schoolwide participation in the effort. He recollects that his job at the time was to facilitate the process and maintain the focus. The superintendent's job was to provide the resources, the most important of which was time. The school used two of the four state-provided institute days and five early-release half-days to support the initiative. In addition, teachers could request additional released time to complete their work. Dufour emphasizes the importance of allocating time:

> We wanted to eliminate the excuse of "we don't have enough time to finish the project." This sent a clear message regarding the importance we placed on the endeavor. It is my observation that too often schools say something is important and then say do it on your own time or after school. I believe if the work is really important we need to provide the time and resources to make it work.

45

Department chairs served as content experts and were responsible for locating resources, leading the study sessions, and developing consensus regarding the outcomes. Typically, a team leader emerged for each specific course, DuFour says, creating additional opportunities for teacher leadership. "For the individual classroom teacher the expectation was that he or she would participate in a collaborative and thoughtful way. You absolutely couldn't elect not to participate."

Teams continue to spend time each year analyzing student performance data, reevaluating course outcomes, building improvement plans, and designing ways to provide individual assistance to students. Measures of student success serve as the primary evidence to determine the impact of staff development. The vision is student focused, and staff development is the vehicle for achieving it.

In 1994, when the district initiated a study of technology, it also focused on student achievement. "A faculty task force examined the current state of the technology in the district, clarified the best thinking, asked what our graduates should be able to do, and then developed a series of recommendations for the district focus," DuFour explains. The report called for significant expenditures for hardware was well as the staff development that would ensure that the technology benefited students. "The staff development design ensured the training component would be based in the workplace rather than in workshops," DuFour says.

DuFour believes the process of curriculum and instructional improvement has become so institutionalized at Adlai Stevenson High School that teachers no longer view it as staff development but simply as "the way we do things around here." He quotes from one of his favorite books, Charles Garfield's *Peak Performers:* "Peak performers in all walks of life find out what they need to learn to advance to their next goal and then set out to learn it." DuFour knows that the students of Adlai Stevenson High School are beneficiaries of this collective effort.

## Jefferson County Public Schools

The Jefferson County Public Schools in Louisville, Kentucky, is an urban district covering about 400 square miles. Its 94,000 students, 30 percent of whom are African American, are served by 6,000 professional staff working in more than 150 schools. To promote middle-level reform, the school district in 1988 established a partnership with the Edna McConnell Clark Foundation Program for Student Achievement. "As a result of this program, after four years of intensive experimentation, study, dialogue, and staff development, we finally can show positive results in terms of middle school reform and student achievement," says Howard Hardin, director for Clark Foundation projects. The project staff includes Hardin, a full-time middle school coalition coordinator, four Clark teaching fellows, a resource assistant, and six part-time parent support coordinators.

The fellows and the parent support coordinators are an indication of the changes the project has brought to the district. The four Clark fellows, who are subject-specific resource persons, work with teachers in language arts, math, science, and social studies. These positions were conceived after the district had gained some experience in middle-level reform as a result of the Clark grant. "Teachers kept saying they didn't want to be pulled from classrooms too much," Hardin recalls. As a result, the district began to provide classroom-based support to its teachers. Clark fellows help teachers focus on curriculum and implement newly written content standards, Hardin explains. They facilitate implementation of the standards through school-based training sessions, study groups, observation and other forms of follow-up, demonstration lessons, peer coaching, small group discussions, and Saturday Seminars.

The parent support coordinators work with parents to help them understand academic standards and what students are actually learning. These coordinators, most of them parents from the community, divide their time among 12 of the district's 24 middle schools. "Parent support coordinators help parents carry on conversations that go beyond how their children are doing in class to what they are learning, what they need to learn, whether teachers are teaching what children need to learn, and whether there's anything else they can do to ensure their children's learning," Hardin says.

Over the past several years the Clark Foundation grant has served as the impetus for the clarification of middle school standards, and both the curriculum and assessment departments are working with schools to develop the standards that now drive instruction. Standards are broken down into guidelines for grade levels; performance standards have also been written for each standards indicator. A similar process has been initiated at the elementary and high school levels. "In the process we have ensured the alignment of local standards with state tests and the national measures of academic progress," Harden points out.

Principals are responsible for monitoring teachers' teaching to standards, Hardin says. Principals meetings provide opportunities for small-group discussions that focus on instructional issues. A three-day summer institute for principals and teachers to facilitate deeper understanding of the standards is another aspect of the district's focus on improved student learning.

Hardin attributes some of the improvement in student learning to a more focused approach to staff development. "Six years ago we had menu-driven programs with no focus for staff development. We had to be more directive and provide for coordination within and across schools," he says. "One thing we have learned in our five years with the Clark Foundation grant is that you have to have common training with a common language and that there has to be commitment from an entire staff toward a common mission."

In addition to these efforts, every school in the district is required under the Kentucky Education Reform Act to develop a transformation plan that focuses on student achievement, the implementation of standards, and the provision of a safe school climate. Monitoring progress on student performance, however, is a challenge, Hardin says, because the state test results don't come back in a timely fashion; the results for spring testing, for example, are not released until the following winter.

The goal of the Clark project is to have 50 percent of the students at the "proficient" or "distinguished" levels by the year 2001. Since 1992 the district has achieved substantial gains in mathematics, with lesser improvements shown in reading and writing, Hardin says. Science test scores, he notes, have been resistant to change.

In addition to these improvements in student learning, Hardin reports other signs of success:

> Students work actively in classrooms; parents show increased interest in what is happening in school; and teachers work smarter and feel less defeated in their work, have more hope for their students, and believe that they can make a difference. Prior to Clark there was a blaming of students and parents and themselves. Today there is hope and belief that

we can more effectively help students achieve academic standards by the time they leave the 8th grade.

## Teachers Academy for Mathematics and Science

Since 1991, students at 65 Chicago schools working with the city's Teachers Academy for Mathematics and Science (TAMS) have made significant gains on the Illinois Goals Assessment Program test in mathematics. They are closing the gap between the Chicago Public Schools and schools in the rest of the state, even surpassing the statewide average in some cases. The academy's long-term professional development for teachers is paying dividends in ways that demonstrate the impact teachers can have on student achievement when they are given the proper tools and skills they need in the classroom, according to Lourdes Monteagudo, TAMS executive director.

TAMS was established in 1991 as an autonomous alliance of leaders from education, government, science and mathematics, business, and the community. The mission of the alliance, Monteagudo says, is to establish collaboration that will ensure excellence in teaching and learning mathematics and science, so that every graduate of Chicago schools is equipped with the knowledge, skills, and competencies to function and contribute meaningfully in a global society.

"The Chicago public schools are a $2.8-billion enterprise and the second-largest employer in the Chicago area," Monteagudo says. "While we cannot afford to retool every teacher, the academy is currently working with more than 2,500 teachers, which makes us equivalent to the third-largest school district in the state."

Joe Frattaroli, chief operating officer of TAMS, says that the academy is guided by a strategic plan. "We conduct a critical reexamination of ourselves and our entire strategic plan every six months," he notes. "We walk through our key values. We review our indicators for our values. We continually seek feedback, and we maintain continuous evaluation of all programs."

To accomplish its mission the academy leverages its experience, expertise, and autonomy to facilitate change, Frattaroli says. TAMS provides a comprehensive school development process that engages the school in the strategic rethinking, revitalizing, and restructuring of its instructional program in mathematics, science, and technology. Focusing on the schools as the unit of change, on teachers as the key change agents, and on all other stakeholders in the school community as agents of support, the school development process focuses on content-driven staff development, organization development, technical assistance, school-community partnerships, and network facilitation.

The academy's efforts have paid off for the Chicago students served by the program, Frattaroli says. Third graders in academy schools received an average score of 157 on the Illinois Goals Assessment Program test in 1992, placing them 104 points behind the state average. By 1995, these schools had an average score of 199, closing the gap to 76 points. The 42-point gain for academy schools is three times the statewide gain of 14 points.

In 1995 the Chicago public schools announced a watch list of schools that had failed to meet state standards for three years, Frattaroli explains. These schools are eligible for intervention assistance under new school reform legislation. Twenty academy schools were on the list. After one year those schools averaged a 14-point gain in the 3rd grade compared with a 3-point gain by other Chicago public schools on the list. In December 1995, when Chicago released its second academic watch list, the number of academy schools on the list had dropped to 14, and no new academy schools had been added.

"There are several elements that have led to our success," Frattaroli points out. "Probably the most important is the support provided teachers at their school sites. The academy is well aware of the critical role of on-the-job support." Each academy staff member is assigned five teachers for follow-up after the off-site training. Frattaroli describes the support in greater detail:

> For example, if one school has 10 teachers participate in training, an academy staff member will spend two days a week at the school for one semester. During that time the academy coach will observe teaching, coteach, provide resources, and help with planning. They provide a safety net in case a lesson falls apart. They are there for debriefing purposes as well.

Frattaroli says that a second strength of TAMS is its commitment to content-driven professional development. "Too many programs are very heavy on process with a weak connection to the content," he explains.

A third element of TAMS's success is its approach to the school improvement process. "We recognize we can't have long-term impact on teachers who teach in dysfunctional situations," Frattaroli says. Consequently, TAMS consultants work with the school leadership team to ensure organizational support and alignment between curriculum and instruction.

Another essential aspect of the program is its parent component. "We have three people working with parents in the schools to ensure their support for learning," Frattaroli says. "We want the parents to understand what is good math and science education and help parents see the power of learning. We know that many parents were not success-ful in school either, so we are trying to accommodate for that as well."

Frattaroli concludes with this observation:

> It is most satisfying to demonstrate the link between professional devel-opment and student outcomes. The investment in quality teaching is the most important investment we can make. All educators need the oppor-tunity for continuous improvement. I believe professional development will be the major educational issue of the 21st century.

# 6

---

# Job-Embedded Learning

Traditionally the dominant form of staff development in most school districts has been either training or large-group awareness sessions. Teachers and administrators leave their jobs to attend workshops that may range from an hour or two to several days spread over a number of months. Critics have long argued that this "sit and get" form of staff development, in which educators are passive recipients of received wisdom from an "expert," has produced little lasting change in the classroom. This type of staff development could also be thought of as "go and get" because "learning" has typically meant leaving the job to participate in the event.

Job-embedded learning, on the other hand, links learning to the immediate and real-life problems faced by teachers and administrators. It is based on the assumption that the most powerful learning is that which occurs in response to challenges currently being faced by the learner and that allows for immediate application, experimentation, and adaptation on the job. In the future, the amount of time devoted to training will diminish, and teachers and administrators will spend most of their learning time in various forms of job-embedded activities.

While well-designed training programs followed by coaching will continue to be the preferred method for the development of certain skills, other types of staff development are becoming increasingly more common as we have come to realize that adult learning can take many forms and use various processes. Sparks and Loucks-Horsley (1989) have identified "five models of teacher development": training, individually guided, observation and feedback, involvement in an improvement process, and inquiry. School employees can also learn through such diverse means as action research, participating in study groups or small-group problem solving, observing peers, planning lessons with colleagues, and journal writing. The San Diego Unified School District in California, the Tucson Unified School District in Arizona, and the Carrollton Farmers Branch Independent School District in Texas provide three examples of job-embedded staff development.

## San Diego Unified School District

The San Diego Unified School District is the eighth-largest urban school district in the United States, with nearly 140,000 students in grades K–12. Approximately 17 percent of those students are African American, 18 percent are Asian (predominantly Filipino and Indochinese), 31 percent are Hispanic, 32 percent are white, and 2 percent are from other ethnic groups. More than 26 percent of the students, who collectively speak more than 60 languages, are classified English-language learners. The district operates more than 180 facilities and employs 6,500 teachers and 700 managers and supervisors.

According to Mary Hopper, instructional team leader, the district's organization and professional development is coordinated through the High Performance in Teaching and Learning Department. Hopper reports to the deputy superintendent. The department includes a specialist for high performance in teaching and learning, 14 resource teachers, and 3 organization development specialists. The resource staff is housed at Dana Center, which serves as a meeting site and also houses curriculum and program support staff personnel.

"Everyone's role in the department is changing as we move away from traditional stand-up training and into more organization development work," Hopper observes. "The department's work is guided by a policy statement, a professional development belief statement, the current district vision and mission, and 16 expectations determined by our superintendent." The Professional Development Policy Statement states the following:

The Board of Education recognizes that in the education of children, the district's most important resource is its employees. In acknowledgment of this, the board working through the administration commits to provide professional development opportunities that focus on enhancing and improving student achievement; support the district's mission, vision, goals, expectations and policies; support site- and department-identified priorities as they relate to improving student achievement and organizational effectiveness; and address various levels of learning.

Mariam True, the department specialist for high performance in teaching and learning, says that a recently acquired Rockefeller Foundation grant for redefining professional development infrastructures in urban districts will allow the system to expand its definition and its services. The Rockefeller initiative has five components that are designed to support job-embedded learning: colloquia, symposia, a cadre of teacher leaders, a Common Ground Town Meeting, and governance.

Colloquia are gatherings of scholars who engage in dialogue, research, and discussion related to a field of study. The department facilitates two-day colloquia held on weekends to address an issue of importance to a particular school or cluster of schools. The two days of work blend the study of research and best practice, discussion of current knowledge, and simulated action research. "As a result of the colloquia we hope the participants return to school with a better understanding of the direction they will take on a particular school priority as well as strategies for continuing the dialogue on the job," True says.

Symposia on the topic of time for staff development are the second component of the Rockefeller initiative. The symposia will explore innovative strategies currently in use as well as create new approaches to finding time for reflection and professional development. "We recognize if we are to make job-embedded learning a reality we have to help people grapple with the issue of time," Hopper explains. "We have a great many schools finding time in unique ways, and we want to showcase these options as well," she adds.

A cadre of 75 teacher leaders will serve as the core of a new Learning Community Network. The cadre will receive intensive training in the areas of group process, facilitation skills, action research, and implementing change so that they may facilitate the development of learning communities in all district schools. "The cadre will help us continue to shift the paradigm on how we develop and deliver staff development," Hopper notes.

Plans also call for hosting a Common Ground Town Meeting, the fourth component of the Rockefeller initiative. This meeting will serve to develop common understandings regarding teaching and learning and a strategic vision for professional development, Hopper explains. The final component will involve a broad representation of stakeholders in reassessing the district's professional development governance structure.

Beyond the Rockefeller initiative, Hopper lists a number of additional structures and programs that demonstrate the district's support for job-embedded learning. Individual schools use eight nonstudent days in various ways to support improved student achievement. All elementary schools also take advantage each week of shortened instructional days. "The schools use the days and released time to work on their goals for student achievement," Hopper says. A number of staff development models, including action research, curriculum development, independent inquiry, and group meetings, are used to achieve school goals.

Eight San Diego schools have used this additional time to support study groups. Through a collaborative effort between the San Diego County Office of Education and the district, these eight sites participated in intensive training to support the development of whole-school study groups that meet weekly to examine ways to improve student achievement. "The schools found a number of creative ways to make time available. For example, one high school divided the eight nonstudent days into one-hour blocks spread throughout the year," explains True, who initiated the project when she worked for the county service center.

San Diego also supports leadership development through job-embedded mentoring. A local university hires retired administrators to provide on-the-job support to newly promoted administrators. "They have absolutely no evaluation responsibility and can thus serve as a real support to our new administrators," Hopper says. These veteran administrators also facilitate the districtwide networking of new administrators.

Another form of job-embedded learning, mentoring of new teachers, received its impetus from state legislation that mandated support for new teachers. New teachers receive on-the-job assistance from both a mentor teacher and a university coach. "This structure has ensured a successful induction year for a large number of our teachers," True observes.

The district has also found a job-embedded solution to its shortage of bilingual teachers, Hopper says. The district hires individuals with bachelor's degrees interested in becoming bilingual teachers. They receive 80 percent of a teacher's salary; the other 20 percent is used to pay for on-the-job support from a mentor and additional training. "The district has found it a successful means for meeting a real need," Hopper says. Using the bilingual experience as a bridge to a larger picture of staff development, Hopper has this to say:

> This is the essence of our role in the district. We are constantly reassessing the resources and support that we need to provide. With our focus clearly on the district vision and mission, we will do whatever it takes to assist teachers and managers to raise student achievement in San Diego.

## Tucson Unified School District

The Tucson Unified School District (TUSD) operates 107 schools and serves 62,000 students, 51 percent of whom are minority, including a 30 percent Hispanic enrollment. Carole Schmidt, the district's director of professional development, reports that before her appointment in 1990, the staff development department consisted of two support staff members in the personnel department who managed the recertification process for the district's 3,000 certified employees. "At that time all staff development was an individual's choice, and secretaries had the authority to approve individuals' selection of conferences for credit and to ensure substitutes were available to cover classes for teachers attending workshops," she recalls.

In 1990, according to Schmidt, the district began a systemwide planning initiative to gain community consensus regarding the profile of a 21st-century graduate, culminating in ACTion 2000, which delineates quality standards for instruction, curriculum, environment, diversity appreciation, home and community partnerships, human resources, leadership, organizational management, assessment, and planning. The eight quality standards are the performance standards that help TUSD measure progress toward achievement of the profile of the 21st-century graduate. "ACTion 2000 became the management, planning, and assessment vehicle that would ensure the profile was realized for Tucson graduates," Schmidt recalls. Concurrently, the district created a strategic plan for staff development.

The combination of ACTion 2000 and the strategic planning process for staff development provided a rationale for making the shift from individually directed staff development to a program focused on district and school goals. ACTion 2000 requires that a leadership team in each school develop a schoolwide action plan for addressing the district standards. Staff development plans are submitted to the assistant superintendent and the staff development department. The district provides support in terms of training, help with meeting facilitation, funding to bring outside expertise to the school, and arranging for individuals to get specialized training.

"In the beginning, most of the plans were what Glickman refers to as 'tinkering at the edges of school improvement,'" Schmidt says. "They were a long list of activities far removed from the issues of instructional improvement. We quickly recognized we had our work cut out for us."

To help schools achieve the goals specified by ACTion 2000, Schmidt recalls, TUSD developed a teacher cadre to provide high-quality school-based training and to serve as meeting facilitators. Initially, courses on such topics as brain-based learning and classroom management were offered in the summer and after school. The cadre also provided training in the core curriculum areas designated as key to achieving the objectives of ACTion 2000. By the second year, the cadre received more requests for whole-school training, as well as for the facilitation of meetings. "The teacher cadre is recognized for delivering high-quality staff development and is a valued source of professional development for teachers and administrators," Schmidt observes.

The cadre also helps school leadership teams understand the qualities of effective staff development and what it takes to produce substantive change in schools, Schmidt says. In addition, the cadre provides training and technical assistance in consensus decision making, facilitation, and team building. As more central office administrators recognized the need to help school leadership teams understand the relationship between staff development and student learning, the district formed an organization development department to assist with the change process.

In an effort to provide staff development that resulted in improved student learning, the organization and staff development departments worked with the district's curriculum specialists to organize an integrated curriculum and instruction institute. School teams, which must include principals, apply to be part of the four-day institute. The program includes large-group instruction as well as time for team planning. Facilitators assist the teams with their planning. Each team produces a plan that describes what will happen at the school and the follow-up support that the professional development department has agreed to provide. The follow-up includes Saturday sessions, whole-school training, and study group and meeting facilitation. "As a result of the institute, we have seen an increase in requests from all schools for staff development," Schmidt says. "Additionally, we've had to expand the number of people who are available to provide follow-up to the institutes."

In addition to school-based training and the districtwide institute, the department also helps design and deliver the staff development critical to the initiatives of other departments. As an example, Schmidt describes how her department has been consulted on numerous occasions to assist with the design of staff development related to an equity lawsuit in the 20 schools named in the settlement.

Another outcome of ACTion 2000 and the staff development strategic plan is a leadership academy for developing teacher leadership and increasing teacher empowerment. "This is not a training ground for administrators," Schmidt says, "but rather an opportunity to come together on a regular basis to inquire into practice, examine the whole notion of leadership, and to identify ways that understanding impacts practice." The academy members meet twice a month over a six-month period. The first session is a discussion of a preassigned reading; the second meeting each month includes a guest speaker, usually from within the school system. At the end of the experience, participants develop a leadership portfolio that is presented to the group. Facilitators are always chosen from the graduating class of the previous year. More than 175 teachers have attended the academy, and 25 have been placed in administrative positions.

TUSD's staff development department also coordinates the new-teacher induction process for the school system. New teachers meet monthly to address typical concerns. They spend part of each meeting in study groups facilitated by members of the teacher cadre. In addition, cadre members provide school-based support to the new teachers.

The staff development department also handles districtwide staff development priorities. To address the issue of diversity, for example, Schmidt reports that she is working with representatives from the departments of African American Studies, Bilingual Education, and Native American Studies to design and deliver staff development. As she explains,

> We try to expose other departments to new models of staff development. In this instance we have had a lot of success addressing issues of diversity through case studies. We offer the process skills assistance, and the consultants in the various departments help us identify the issues for discussion. It is a comfortable collaboration that benefits everyone in the school district.

Schmidt predicts that the staff development department will continue to rely on its strengths in bringing together groups with a common agenda to study, plan, and act on behalf of the students of Tucson:

> Our success lies in our ability to provide powerful examples of what needs to happen in our schools. As we model the effectiveness of collaboration in central office, we help build capacity in schools so that teachers are responsible for their own learning. We believe that everyone in the organization needs to be a learner.

## Carrollton Farmers Branch Independent School District

Carrollton Farmers Branch Independent School District (CFB) in suburban Dallas serves 20,500 students on 27 campuses. Linda Hawkins, principal at Davis Elementary School, expresses her pride in the school system's commitment to excellence: "We are a school system that remains on the cutting edge of learning with a focus on improving success for all children."

Cognitive coaching, a tool to promote teacher reflection, is used in more than two-thirds of CFB's schools as an alternative to a more traditional teacher evaluation system mandated by the Texas Education

Agency. The district views cognitive coaching as a key strategy for improving student success in a school system that views staff development from a systemic perspective.

In 1986 Kathy Harwell, the district's former staff development director, and Linda Hawkins attended a session on cognitive coaching led by Robert Garmston and Peg Luiden at a regional education service center. "I loved the program because it was so consistent with my view of myself as a principal who facilitates the learning of others," Hawkins says. As a result, Harwell and Hawkins integrated cognitive coaching into the district's Effective Teaching Training program.

Later, when Harwell assumed additional responsibility for a districtwide teacher evaluation that used a traditional process, she commented to Hawkins, "This is crazy. Why are we using a process that doesn't appear to facilitate growth when we know a better process that we could substitute for it?" Following that discussion, Harwell and Hawkins approached the superintendent with a request to use cognitive coaching as an alternative to the Texas Teacher Appraisal System.

As a result, a committee of staff development and teacher evaluation experts from across the state of Texas studied the implications of replacing the traditional teacher appraisal system with cognitive coaching. Ultimately, the state education agency approved a waiver from the state-mandated system, and the school board approved a pilot program in two schools. A three-year evaluation design was then developed to measure the impact of cognitive coaching on teacher behavior and student learning.

The philosophy behind cognitive coaching is that students' higher-level thinking skills will be improved if teachers' own skills are enhanced through cognitive coaching. "We can't expect teachers to help children practice metacognition skills if they haven't been provided the support to develop those skills for themselves," Hawkins says.

The process for teachers begins when they attend a voluntary, district-sponsored, four-day training program. Afterward they are offered the option of using cognitive coaching in place of the traditional teacher evaluation process. Following the training, responsibility for implementation shifts to the school. The principal selects a coach from a list of three to five names submitted by the teacher. The coaching partners meet at the beginning of the school year; teachers write three goals that are aligned with the professional competencies established by the Texas Education Agency. The first goal must address some aspect of student achievement. The second goal focuses on the metacognitive development of the teacher. The third goal addresses the teacher's professional development needs. "Goals are established by teachers in alignment with the teacher competencies dictated by the state education agency," Hawkins says. "However, most teachers also recognize the importance of aligning their individual goals with the district's and school's improvement plans."

Following the establishment of the goals, the coaching partners meet with the principal to review the plan. The principal or alternate supervisor helps in the development of action steps and assessment strategies, a process that typically takes about three hours. "This is not a time-saving process for principals looking for an alternative to the traditional evaluation process," Hawkins notes, "but rather a very effective process for anyone interested in strengthening instruction."

The coaching pair meets a minimum of eight times per year and has a conference with the supervisor at the midway point. The supervisor also conducts "walk throughs" to provide nonjudgmental observational feedback. Later the coaching pair meets with the supervisor in another three-hour conference to review documentation and create a summative statement that reflects in the teacher's own words his or her learning for the year. At the conclusion of the meeting, the coach leaves and the teacher ranks himself or herself on a matrix rating scale closely aligned with the state's teacher proficiencies and on the skills developed in cognitive coaching. The district provides continuous support for the effort. Follow-up meetings and ongoing training are scheduled in the fall and spring of each of the three years after the initial training. At the end of each year, the University of North Texas completes an external evaluation. During the first and second year, evaluation surveys provide opportunities for teachers to reflect on the impact of the process on their performance. Hawkins notes the positive response:

> It is not uncommon to hear teachers comment as early as the second semester on the impact of the process in terms of their confidence in their questioning of students, their responses to student reactions to alternative methods of assessment, and on language pattern differences used in parent conferences.

By the end of the third year teachers are asked to examine the impact of their changed behavior on their students. Recent research validated the impact the process has had on students' ability in developing higher-order thinking skills. According to Harwell, the former staff development director and champion of cognitive coaching, the process encourages and motivates persons of all ages to think for themselves, to question and extend their own thinking as well as that of others, and to help children achieve at higher levels. "When we inquire into our own practice, we find many ways to create greater success for all children," she says.

As assistant superintendent in the nearby Grapevine-Colleyville Independent School District, Harwell is using cognitive coaching as a process for administrator appraisal. "This process is directly related to the practice, application, and modeling of the skills required of instructional leaders," she says. "'Walking the talk' has never had greater meaning than when used to describe the alignment and promotion of thinking skills throughout the system for students and staff alike."

# 7

## The Study of Teaching and Learning

In the past a staff development event—a workshop, for example—
was the final step in a long chain of events. Researchers had studied
the topic and written reports of their work, trainers had examined
the research or worked with the researchers, and the staff development
program was designed by district or school leaders. The last step in this
series saw teachers entering a workshop in which they often were
relatively passive recipients of the researchers' knowledge and the trainers' expertise. Teachers then returned to their classrooms and implemented what they had "learned" with varying degrees of success. Most
often, little evidence of use could be found even a few months after the
program's conclusion.

Recently teachers have more frequently become engaged in the
ongoing study of the teaching/learning process. Faculties have divided
themselves into study groups of six to eight persons that meet weekly
for an hour or more to discuss research they have read on how the human
brain learns, on cognitive psychology, and on various methods for
improving instruction. They discuss the credibility of the research and
its implications for their school and classrooms.

Teachers are also engaging in action research (Calhoun 1994) in
which they identify teaching/learning issues of importance, try out new
methods, and determine their effect on students learning. The results of

the investigation often trigger another round of investigation. In addition, teachers are more often planning lessons with colleagues or as part of teaching teams. Teachers may plan the lesson together, coteach the lesson, and analyze its effectiveness. The Madison Metropolitan School District in Wisconsin and the Valley Stream Union School District 313 in New York provide examples of such inquiry.

## Madison Metropolitan School District

The Madison Metropolitan School District (MMSD) serves approximately 24,000 students in 29 elementary schools, 9 middle schools, and 4 high schools. A strategic plan guides district improvements. According to Cathy Caro-Bruce, a staff and organization development specialist in the district, the mission of the district's staff and organization development team is "to ensure student and staff success through the application of continuous improvement standards and practices." It provides "ongoing training/development, facilitation, and consultation, which enable MMSD employees to achieve increasingly better results in terms of the mission and objectives of the district and its schools, support systems, programs, and services." The department is composed of a coordinator of staff and organization development, who reports to the deputy superintendent; and three other staff development specialists in addition to Caro-Bruce.

The adoption of a district strategic plan elevated the importance of staff development, Caro-Bruce notes. "The district is adding 1.5 new staff developers to address the changing needs of the district, and this is practically unheard of." She believes that the growth "is based on what we've accomplished and the recognition of the need to continue our restructuring efforts focused on teaching and learning."

Within the context of the district plan, the department is charged with the responsibility of ensuring continuous quality improvement. One of the department's efforts, a classroom action research pilot project begun in the mid-1980s, has become one of the most effective staff development strategies for facilitating the process of continuous quality improvement. In 1990 Caro-Bruce was successful in linking the process with major district initiatives.

Caro-Bruce describes the first such link, which emerged from a two-year-old district-sponsored project on "Cultural Differences and

Classroom Strategies." The project teaches elementary school teachers strategies to help them succeed with an increasingly diverse clientele. The project's third year was designated for institutionalization and assessment. Seeing a possible link, Caro-Bruce suggested action research as a tool for helping teachers reflect on the strategies they were implementing and to determine the project's impact. She recalls the situation:

> For the first time there was a source of funding and an organizational connection to action research. This connection was critical to getting started in the district. For years I wanted people to have this experience because it was something inherently worth doing; but in retrospect, I recognize that for people to buy in, they had to see that it would make a difference for children in their classrooms and for them as individuals.

According to Caro-Bruce, action research by teachers and principals has gradually become part of the culture of the school system, and the process itself continues to evolve. The process involves identification of a problem or question by each participant, examination and assessment of individual work for the purpose of considering changes in behavior, and collaboration with course facilitators and other participants. Three general expectations are set for all participants: attend meetings regularly, participate in discussions, and write about findings.

An action research process cycle takes an entire school year and is orchestrated to encourage the continuous involvement of all participants, as Caro-Bruce makes clear:

> The primary expectation for that year is that each participant will focus on some aspect of teaching and learning. You need to start with yourself if you really want to make changes to help children. Selecting the appropriate question is the biggest challenge. The process participants go through forces them to think about their work differently. The questions of other members push people to move to the next step in their work.

A facilitator helps the group identify criteria for good questions and modify individual questions as necessary. Past participants have studied topics as diverse as increasing the achievement of African American students, encouraging self-reflection by students, promoting student ownership of learning, understanding the impact of teachers remaining with students for two consecutive years, and determining key factors in effective classroom discipline.

The group is taught various research methods and data collection techniques. A considerable amount of library research time is scheduled as well. Caro-Bruce explains the process further:

> Throughout the action research process, participants discuss problems, issues, concerns, insights, and observations emerging from their inquiry. The process can be never ending as action researchers continuously plan, act, observe, reflect, plan, act, and so on. Participants are expected to reflect on their experiences and prepare a written report based on their work.

Caro-Bruce points out that although anecdotal evidence has pointed to the many benefits teachers derive from their participation in action research, until recently the district had not taken a systematic look at the impact of action research on teachers. In 1995 the district, in collaboration with the University of Wisconsin, received a MacArthur Spencer Professional Development Grant to examine the impact of action research on teachers' thinking, their practice, and student learning. "Participants have told us that they perceive us as organized, nonthreatening, and enthusiastic, and that they appreciate the opportunity the district is providing them," Caro-Bruce observes. A number of teachers have published the results of their work and have made presentations at conferences throughout the United States. "The teachers tell us they have become more reflective in their work, they have grown professionally, and the process has lead to further learning," Caro-Bruce says. "Once people see the various ways they can use action research, they take it in many more directions than I would have ever anticipated."

Caro-Bruce says that the district is considering broadening action research to address school improvement plans and whole-school change. "I wouldn't want to let go of individual action research projects, however, because of the richness of what happens when you put together a group of people who don't work in the same school," she argues. "There's an exchange that occurs that is different than when a school looks at one particular issue." She goes on to describe the potential of action research to influence change:

> Real restructuring is going to require the principles inherent in action research—identifying the important questions, collecting data to learn about our questions, reflecting on what was learned, and taking action

based on that learning. When this pattern becomes embedded in the culture of a school, you will see a healthy, self-renewing organization, willing to embrace the changes that the future holds. For me, the most exciting part is when teachers begin to have a discussion about issues regarding change, and they talk about what questions they have and what data they need to collect. They begin to see data as helpful and critical to their decisions. Action research is driving the way teachers are looking at restructuring in their schools so that it benefits their students.

## Valley Stream Union School District #313

Martin Brooks is superintendent of the Valley Stream Union School District #313, an elementary school district serving 2,080 students in suburban New York City. As he began his tenure in the district in 1992 he quickly heard from many sources that the quality of the district's program no longer matched its fine reputation. As a result, Brooks set up a series of "cracker-barrel meetings" in which he visited the district's four elementary schools to gather staff perceptions of needs. "Teachers expressed their frustration at not being able to learn to do what they were reading about in journals," he recounts. "They said, for instance, that they were being asked to implement a whole-language approach but weren't being provided any support to do so."

Brooks next set up meetings with parents to see if they held similar views. He quickly learned that the community felt the schools had a well-meaning, competent staff who had fallen behind because of the school district's lack of investment in their professional development.

The district needed a comprehensive approach to staff development if it was to move back up to the level it had once occupied, Brooks concluded. "I am a strong proponent of staff development. The human resources we have are our most important ones. I wanted to set the process into motion."

As a result, in his first "state of the district" report, Brooks established goals for curriculum development, instructional improvement, and structural changes. Staff development became the vehicle for addressing these topics and for achieving the district's 26 goals.

Several years before his appointment to Valley Stream, Brooks and his wife, Jackie, had developed an interest in constructivism. He explains the major ideas behind constructivism:

Its basic message is that human beings, regardless of age, learn best when they have the opportunity to construct meaning for themselves. Constructivism is based on the philosophy that quality education taps the experiential base of the learner. It uses the questions and hypothesis of the learner as the basis for more learning. So much of the curriculum in schools is presented as part to whole; it assumes that once children get all the parts they can create the whole. But this doesn't happen. In reality we learn whole to part. Think about how we assemble bicycles: we see the drawing and use it as a guide as we insert slot A in B.

Brooks recognized that much of the staff was not oriented to the philosophy of constructivist teaching and learning. He recalls seeking a point of entry:

As luck would have it, concerns were being expressed about the science textbooks, which in turn led to the development of a districtwide committee that moved in its discussion from the issue of what to do about a shortage of textbooks to broaden conversations about what to do with science in the elementary grades and how to develop a more hands-on experimental approach.

As members of the committee spent two summers rewriting the science curriculum, the district used curriculum development to begin constructivist teaching of science.

To interest others in the new approach, Brooks began leading a series of workshops in the district. "I tried to plant ideas and to find ways for people to talk about them," Brooks says. Because constructivism requires a major shift in the behaviors of teachers and students, Brooks understood that it was not something that could be mandated. Participants needed the opportunity to reflect on the kinds of changes the shift would demand and to be able to ask tough questions. With the superintendent leading the sessions, district support for the initiative was clear.

Brooks next invited groups to identify obstacles to the institutionalization of constructivist teaching and learning. The identified obstacles included an overemphasis on national norm-referenced testing, report cards with letter grades, existing methods of communicating with parents, and current state assessment measures.

According to Brooks, the district found ways to address each obstacle and to align practice with the new philosophy of teaching. For example, report cards were changed to include checklists and narrative comments, and the number of parent conferences was doubled to facilitate greater communication between parents and teachers. At the same time, evening meetings were held with parents so that they could learn about the rationale for making the shift. "By the end of my second year in the district staff members were gravitating to workshops on specific content and to discussions of philosophical principles underlying constructivist teaching," Brooks says.

At about this point in his tenure, Brooks became aware that the district staff was sending a message to slow the pace of change. "I said I wouldn't do that," he recalls. "I was being told that I should choose a single initiative or curriculum area and stick with it for two or three years." Brooks responded by saying that he believed offering teachers a number of initiatives for consideration was critical. He argued that if only one initiative was offered for a three-year period, it might not appeal to a large enough segment of his staff; on the other hand, if a number of initiatives were offered, no one could have an excuse for not participating. "As long as all initiatives are undergirded with the same philosophy, it doesn't matter how many are offered, and everyone doesn't need to feel obligated to attempt everything," he says

Because Brooks recognized that example is a powerful teacher, staff development sessions designed to teach constructivism are themselves based on constructivist principles. In these sessions adults are given meaningful tasks, with debriefings linked to the classroom. Brooks describes a staff development activity he uses that asks participants to read a particular story and to reflect on a series of questions that bring additional meaning to it:

> Next, we slap a worksheet on the overhead with questions such as, what was the main idea? who were the main characters? and other boring questions we typically ask of students. Finally, we ask participants to compare how they felt with the two sets of tasks and to discuss how their students might feel.

The district is still in a state of transition in its shift to a constructivist approach. Brooks says that although the constructivist train is on the track and many are taking the ride, some remain resistant to boarding. His challenge is to find the right balance of pressure and support. A comprehensive annual assessment that includes interviews with current students, past students, staff members, and parents has convinced him of the need to continue to apply the pressure for change. "For the first time in four years students are using words like *fun* to describe the learning process and complaining about learning through worksheets," Brooks says. "While most of the parents are supportive of the changes, I recognize there are still those who would prefer a more traditional approach to teaching. I need to continue to work with them and not get out too far ahead of any of my parents."

Although the staff remains supportive of the shift, many still want to slow the pace of change. Brooks is adamant, however, about not giving in to that pressure. "In every setting there is a unique and discrete window of opportunity to make change," he observes. "I think it is important for people in leadership positions to see those windows and take advantage of them. Although it is tempting to heed the advice of those asking for the pace of change to be slowed, doing so would not be in the best interests of students or staff."

# 8

## Adding Content-Specific Learning to Generic Approaches

During the 1980s a large portion of staff development involved training on generic instructional skills. Kindergarten through 12th grade teachers—sometimes in the same setting—learned about cooperative learning, learning styles, and the Madeline Hunter approach to teaching, among other topics, in workshops that ranged in length from a few hours to several days. These programs were based on the assumption that all teachers would benefit from learning about and applying one or more aspects of the research on effective teaching.

In the view of some educators, however, this approach did not sufficiently address critical differences between the type of instruction that is most beneficial in various content areas and at different grade levels (Shulman 1986). In addition to urging more focused training in instructional skills, these individuals also argued that teachers need to deepen their knowledge of the content they teach and to understand that content in a way that promotes students' deeper understanding. Because many teachers themselves had been taught their academic disciplines at a relatively superficial level, this process, it was argued, would make it possible for teachers to move their students to deeper levels of understanding. In addition, this deeper understanding would help teachers become aware of and address common misconceptions that students possessed regarding a particular discipline. The Middle Grade Mathematics Renaissance in California and the Teachers Academy for Mathematics and Science in Illinois, described in Chapter 5, illustrate such content-specific staff development.

## The Middle Grade Mathematics Renaissance

The Middle Grade Mathematics Renaissance is a component of the California Alliance for Mathematics and Science, which, in turn, is part of the California Statewide Systemic Initiative. The Math Renaissance works with educators to transform middle grade mathematics and to encourage students to continue their study of mathematics. "The initiative was a response to a need to disseminate and implement a statewide mathematics framework," Renaissance Program Director Judy Mumme says. "Middle grades were chosen as key points for intervention for two reasons. First, projects were already in place in high schools. Second, middle school math is a gatekeeper to students' future success in mathematics."

In addition to Mumme, the Renaissance staff consists of 10 full-time regional directors. The regional directors facilitate work with all schools in their designated region and guide the efforts of cluster leaders who provide on-site assistance to teachers in the project. "Math Renaissance is a school-based improvement initiative," Mumme says. "It requires a heavy financial and personnel investment. By making this investment schools demonstrate their commitment to the goals of the project and their willingness to stick with it over time." Schools pay all teacher stipends, substitute costs for 8 to 12 days per teacher, material costs, and an annual $3,000 participation fee to cover the costs of a local teacher leader. In total, schools invest between $10,000 and $15,000 to participate in the project.

According to Mumme, the middle school math curriculum is a thinking-centered curriculum. Using professional development as its central strategy, the Renaissance focuses on helping schools implement the National Council of Teachers of Mathematics (NCTM) Curriculum and Evaluation Standards, the NCTM Professional Standards for Teaching Mathematics, and the California Mathematics and Science Curriculum Framework.

"The goal is to change the pedagogical and content focus of math instruction in the middle grades by aligning with national standards and the California framework," Mumme explains. As she describes the program, it is

> a long-term, year-around initiative. Participants have at least three years of intensive involvement, which includes 8 to 12 full-day seminars during the academic year and one- to four-week summer experiences such as teaching academies, institutes, or retreats. A minimum of two teachers is expected to participate. By the third year a large proportion of the mathematics faculty is expected to be participating.

One of the most unique and most popular elements of the professional development strategy is the introduction of a "replacement curriculum," Mumme notes. The Renaissance team identifies the most innovative and powerful middle grade curriculum to be found and provides demonstration lessons for participating teachers. Teachers are then asked to replace a chunk of their curriculum with a new unit and observe what happens with their students. If they decide to keep the new curriculum, they have to decide what to throw out in its place. They are expected to describe their reactions in journals, discuss their reactions in classes, and share samples of student work from the replacement unit. "There were exciting benefits as well as problems associated with the replacement curriculum strategy," Mumme observes. "Some teachers liked their students' response so much they began to collect and horde replacement units. They became less interested in the reflection and discussion and more interested in acquiring additional units."

According to Mumme, in order to build capacity at the school the program has become more supportive of site leadership. "We have begun to pull back from doing so much of the work ourselves [and are] putting more in the hands of schools," she says. "We model the way we want teachers to work with other teachers and the way we want teachers to work with students. Walking our talk is critical, so we also invest in the ongoing professional development of the Renaissance staff."

A research team from the Far West Laboratory is evaluating the effectiveness of the Renaissance, Mumme says. Fifty percent of the 130 participating districts have enrolled all of their middle schools in the program. Changes in teacher attitudes and behaviors are being documented, as well as changes in program structures. To date, the research indicates that students in more than 1,000 middle grade classrooms are regularly engaged in cooperative learning and writing and are using concrete materials and calculators to help develop mathematical understanding. Tracking has been reduced in 47 percent of the schools. In addition, more than 300 parent nights have been conducted to enlist parent and community support.

The Renaissance program has reaffirmed that schools need ongoing support to maintain their progress and further their development, and that the process of reform is never ending. "Success also has a lot to do with the view of the school toward the program," Mumme concludes. "If they view it as an expense, chances are it won't continue if support is withdrawn. When they view it as an investment that helps teachers to expand their understanding of teaching and learning, chances are much more likely it will continue."

# 9

## Consultation, Planning, and Facilitation

Fifteen or 20 years ago most staff developers spent a great deal of their time coordinating courses and training sessions. They assessed staff members' needs, hired presenters, and made certain that the presenter, the participants, and the coffee all ended up in the same room at the same time. Beginning in the 1980s many staff developers were hired as trainers in a number of areas, particularly those related to instruction.

As school systems have restructured and moved toward site-based decision making, staff developers are being asked to play new roles. They are more frequently called on to facilitate meetings or to help various work groups (e.g., a school faculty, the superintendent's cabinet, a school improvement team) solve problems or develop long-range plans. They are also asked to train others to serve as consultants, facilitators, and planners. Examples of these new roles for staff developers are provided by the Adams 12 Five Star School District in Colorado, and the Broward County School District and the Lee County Public Schools in Florida.

## Adams 12 Five Star School District

With the advent of decentralization and site-based decision making in the early 1980s, the Adams 12 Five Star School District in Northglenn, Colorado (also described in Chapter 2) soon recognized that traditional staff development programs in instructional skills and curriculum areas would not be sufficient to prepare school system employees for their new responsibilities. As a result, reports Joellen Killion, a staff development trainer in the school system, the district began offering training programs in "process skills" such as conflict management and school improvement techniques (e.g., action planning, data collection, diagnosing, team development, evaluation). She recalls that many people thought they had some skills in such areas as consensus decision making and team building, "but once they found themselves in difficult situations they couldn't make things work. As a result of some chaos we experienced for a year or two, we put together process training programs in some of these areas."

One outcome of these changes was the creation of a facilitator cadre. Initially, cadre members were selected because they were influential in the system and because they represented the various employee groups. The original idea, Killion says, was to develop the facilitation skills of the 15 cadre members so that they could work with groups that were experiencing conflict as they designed new projects or implemented innovations. Soon participants found themselves involved in major district projects, such as reducing the budget or redesigning transportation services. For many years a cadre member facilitated meetings of the superintendent's cabinet. It soon became evident, Killion says, that 15 facilitators were not enough, so more and more were trained each year. Today the district has about 150 trained facilitators.

According to Killion, the staff development department recognizes that it must build the capacity of other people to be staff developers. The department also has had to provide new types of services, such as consultation, coaching, and training the trainer. To illustrate this change, Killion describes a school where she has been a consultant but has never worked directly with the entire staff:

> Two years ago, a principal and assistant principal from an elementary school came to talk over their school's plans for the year. They wanted to renew their plan and get my reaction to the process they were going

through. They wanted to know if anything might be missing. I coached them about how you develop a set of beliefs and why it was important that the beliefs be determined before making decisions about actions. This process within the school became a series of monthly meetings. Each month before each meeting I would go over to the school to help them design the agenda and explore the materials they might need at the meeting. Afterwards they would debrief the meeting with me, sometimes bringing another staff member along to provide the staff's perspective. We would then together determine their next steps. It was a matter of coplanning and designing with them all the steps along the way to get where they wanted to go. This school is now involved in coaching another school through the same process they used.

In Adams 12 consultation and facilitation skills find a wide variety of applications. According to Killion, staff developers are now asked to consult with schools in areas such as data collection, evaluation design, and conflict resolution, among others.

## Broward County Public Schools

The Broward County Public Schools, with more than 200,000 students in approximately 200 schools, is one of the largest and fastest-growing school systems in the country. The Human Resource Development Department (HRD) is responsible for all administrative training, noninstructional staff training, and leadership and pedagogical training for teachers, and for coordinating curriculum training with curriculum staff. In addition, more than 25 departments have some level of responsibility for providing staff development. A Coordination Council managed by Dianne Aucamp, director of human resource development, coordinates all of these efforts. Half of the financial resources for human resource development is allocated at the system level, and the other half goes directly to the schools.

According to Aucamp, the Human Resource Development Department has four functional areas: skills development, organization development, leadership development, and instructional development. Skills development programs provide job-related skills. The organization development function focuses on the link between school improvement and teacher development. The leadership function develops the knowledge, skills, and dispositions associated with effective leadership for both current and aspiring administrators. Also included is teacher leadership training for school-based improvement. The instructional development area focuses on the connection between curriculum and instruction and what needs to occur to ensure that students are taught a demanding curriculum with research-based pedagogy.

"About three years ago we reorganized into these functional areas as opposed to audiences served," Aucamp says. "However, the adjustment was not easy, and the lines are not always clear. For example, the HRD aligns the preparation and ongoing support of substitute teachers with the instructional development function, while a case could also be made to place it under skills development."

In 1994, Frank R. Petruzielo, the district's recently appointed superintendent, established a school accountability process that holds principals accountable for the results of the school improvement process, Aucamp recalls. Twelve indicators of improvement were approved by the school board and endorsed by various stakeholders. During the 1995 school year, baseline data were collected at all schools. Schools have been given three years to improve student performance. If student performance does not improve by the end of the second year, an area assistant superintendent is assigned to work with the school. If improvement does not occur by the end of the third year, the superintendent may take whatever steps are necessary to ensure gains in student learning. "This has caused principals to scurry for services that will make a difference in terms of student achievement," Aucamp says. "We have many more demands for consultation, planning, and instructional training then we have ever seen before. These services are no longer viewed as a luxury by our schools, but rather as an integral part of the school operation."

"The challenge in the Human Resource Department is to provide a coherent and organized picture of all that we have to offer schools to facilitate their achievement of their goals for student success," Aucamp says. "Although we still coordinate or deliver more than 4,000 workshops per year, our role in the Human Resource Department has really expanded beyond the training paradigm."

The department begins by reviewing the more than 200 school improvement plans, analyzing data and needs, and determining its own high-priority areas for services to schools. When new initiatives or needs are uncovered, central office study teams are organized to ensure the district has the knowledge and understanding necessary to provide the leadership and guidance requested by the schools. Similar processes are taught to schools to ensure thorough study of any initiative considered for implementation.

Another department strategy, according to Aucamp, is to facilitate school team involvement with district, state, and national networks. Within the district, 50 schools are associated with the Coalition of Essential Schools, 28 schools are involved with a district initiative on shared decision making, 22 are part of a state network, and 50 schools are involved with TEAMS (Teachers Exploring and Mastering Strategies). The department initiated TEAMS to build school-based systems to facilitate ongoing learning. Initially, core teams from each school were taught instructional processes that would improve student learning. Participants then formed study groups to examine various issues. University faculty members served as coaches as well as critical friends to the study teams. "This initiative has led the schools to recognize the importance of on-the-job, school-based learning," Aucamp says.

The Human Resource Development Department also is responsible for coordinating responses to state and system-level mandates for change. For example, the state has mandated ESOL training for all Florida teachers. The department is responsible for ensuring that more than 1,200 teachers complete training within a two-year time frame. At the system level, the superintendent has selected 11 schools to pilot a 90-minute block schedule, and HRD, working with the curriculum department, is helping the schools with the design, planning, and development of curriculum and instructional strategies.

Aucamp notes another unique service HRD provides to help schools implement their improvement plans. At an annual in-district Schools of Excellence Convention, the department coordinates the concurrent sessions and exhibits of school improvement initiatives within the school system. Staff, parents, and community members are invited to the annual event, which attracts more than 3,500 attendees. "The objective is to share best practice in the district so schools are not reinventing the wheel," Aucamp says.

Although the district appears to be on the right track in providing the variety of services necessary to ensure student success, Aucamp acknowledges there are problems:

The biggest frustration is getting all stakeholders to recognize the importance of job-embedded learning and how it relates to everything they are trying to accomplish. When schools finally get involved and see the results in terms of impact on children, then they are sold. But with a school superintendent who strongly supports staff development we know more schools will discover it as key to their challenge.

## Lee County Public Schools

The Lee County Public School System in Florida serves about 51,000 students on 52 campuses consisting of 36 elementary schools, 12 middle schools, 9 high schools, and 7 vocational and exceptional centers. The student population is 60 percent white and 40 percent minority; 10 percent of the students require ESOL services. The district employs 6,000 persons, including 3,000 teachers, 300 of whom are new to the district each year. According to Stephanie Webb, a teacher on special assignment in the staff development department, "Staff development is the hub of everything that happens in the district. This is because the superintendent was a former resource coordinator in staff development and recognizes the value of staff development." Sharon Benner, the district's director of staff development, adds, "This level of programming and services ensures an important component of support for teachers working in an era of restructuring and change."

The staff development department's organizational home is in the human resources division. It includes a director, a principal on assignment, a coordinator for support personnel, a coordinator for teacher education, and two teachers on special assignment. The principal on assignment, a rotating position, is responsible for principal development and for the leadership development of potential administrators or those who wish to improve their skills as teacher leaders. One teacher on special assignment is responsible for the beginning teacher program, ESOL training, clinical educator training (peer teaching), and the master inservice plan required by the state. The second teacher on assignment is responsible for grant programs and special projects.

Webb outlines the role of staff development in the district:

Staff development is viewed as the pivotal piece to ensure the district achieves the goals of Florida's Blueprint 2000 in concert with local school board goals. A variety of delivery systems help us achieve this. The system has an improvement and growth mentality. It expects its staff developers to stay on the cutting edge in terms of programming for adults and students that will enable the achievement of its goals. Everyone recognizes the need to continuously study and improve. We sometimes feel like we're on a spinning top watching everything and waiting for appropriate openings to provide the kind of service or help that you believe will make the difference for children.

Webb describes the department as having a problem-solving mentality:

Its goal is to find the way staff development can help the customers meet their needs. The department offers what is affectionately referred to as "staff development on demand." Any district crisis can be turned into an opportunity for the staff development department. For example, due to budget cuts, the district has been forced to release bus monitors and replace some of them with video cameras on buses. Staff development has been called on to develop a training program to assist bus drivers with this transition.

The department is quality conscious, Webb notes, and staff members spend a great deal of time debriefing everything they do. "The department is viewed as a place where the brain trust sits, a department of movers and shakers. We have people on staff from 6:30 a.m. until 9:30 p.m. daily. We stagger hours to accommodate our customers."

Webb lists a number of current district-based services: teacher induction, mandated ESOL training, facilitative leadership, Stephen Covey's "Seven Habits," effective teaching, and quality improvement efforts, among others. The district also provides noninstructional and instructional staff career counseling. In addition, the district is known for its annual summer institute series. More than 300 participants from three counties attend the two-week event, and they may earn a maximum of 60 inservice points, the equivalent of three hours of college credit. Schools may send teams or individuals, and participation is voluntary. The series offers institutes ranging from 1 to 10 days in length, with topics identified by schools, the school board, and state mandates. Common topics include curriculum areas such as math and science, as well as the pedagogy of teaching. Course instructors come from within and outside the district. Periodically, keynoters bring the entire group of participants together for a common learning experience. The staff development department evaluates immediate effects and is studying ways to measure long-term results. The department is considering alternative delivery models for the institutes, including training for entire school faculties.

The department also offers year-round technology training guided by a districtwide needs assessment. The department works with a teacher cadre to deliver the custom-designed support to individual campuses. Groups with similar training needs or interests may also come together at a central technology lab.

School-based staff development is another important aspect of the department's work, Webb says. The department receives a copy of each school improvement plan and works directly with individual school inservice representatives to identify campus-based needs. "Schools target individual areas for improvement and may work with the staff development department to broker the hiring of consultants," she explains. "They may also use a member of the department to help with the achievement of campus-based goals. Schools have their own pot of staff development money, and many collaborate with other schools to save money."

The greatest challenge facing the department is serious budget cuts, Webb claims. As a result, the staff development department must decide whether to continue to try to do everything in a quality manner or to take a stand that the job can't be done at the same level of quality with fewer resources. Webb offers this observation:

> The staff developer mentality is to do whatever is asked of you. The days of dog-and-pony shows are over, so we have to take a more systemic look at the needs of the district. Enabling schools to plan effective staff development is one way the central office can respond to reduction in resources while strengthening site-based ownership for professional growth.

# 10

# Spreading Responsibility for Staff Development

In the past most school employees had the luxury of assuming that most staff development responsibilities belonged to someone else. Principals and teachers could look to a central office staff member who planned, coordinated, and sometimes even presented staff development programs. In larger districts that person was often a director or coordinator of staff development. In smaller systems, the assistant superintendent for instruction or the director of curriculum would assume those responsibilities. Whatever the case, it was possible for virtually all district employees to view staff development as someone else's job.

Today, the concept of job-embedded staff development has come to mean that educators in many roles—superintendents, assistant superintendents, curriculum supervisors, principals, and teacher leaders, among others—must *all* see themselves as teachers of adults and must view the development of others as one of their most important responsibilities. These individuals are increasingly being held accountable for their performance as planners and implementers of various forms of staff development.

The spread of responsibility for staff development throughout the school system has hardly diminished the role of the staff development department, however. If anything, staff development departments have become even more important. They are assisting teachers and administrators by offering training and ongoing support in acquiring the necessary knowledge and skills needed in their new responsibilities, such as serving on school improvement teams or mentoring colleagues; by providing one-to-one coaching of these individuals in their new roles; and by facilitating meetings that are best led by individuals who are outside a particular group. Patwin Elementary School in Davis, California, and the Muscogee County School District in Georgia illustrate this expanded view of staff development leadership.

## Patwin Elementary School

Patwin Elementary School, in the Davis Joint Unified School District in California, serves 650 children in kindergarten through 6th grade. Although 70 percent of its students are Caucasian, its location in a university community brings it a diverse student body from Australia, South America, China, Europe, and Iran. "The students' families value education," principal Diane Zimmerman observes. "At the same time, you see in our community expensive homes next to subsidized housing, with not much in between."

Patwin opened in 1991, and Zimmerman was named principal in 1993. In 1994 the staff and members of the community declared that the school's mission was to stimulate creativity and curiosity and to challenge students to reach their highest potential, which is captured in the Patwin slogan, "Everyone teaches, everyone learns." In Zimmerman's words, the Patwin community is

> committed to fostering a love of learning, opening doors for children, creating new connections, and supporting academic success for all within an environment of trust and mutual respect. Patwin strives to provide an environment that is a safe, friendly, joyful place to learn, where children feel free to explore and discover, to experiment with ideas, and to take creative risks. The school fosters a learning community where, with effort and concentration, and with strong home and school support, all children can successfully acquire the skills needed to become lifelong learners. We believe and delight in the unlimited potential of our students. The hawk's flight symbolizes our vision for our children: to soar, to experience joy and freedom, and to apply strength, grace, and a keen eye to a noble purpose.

According to Zimmerman, Patwin demonstrates its commitment to collaboration and shared decision making in many ways. All staff members assume leadership positions and take responsibility for the school program as needed. A Staff Liaison Council, composed of grade-level and special area representatives, solves problems, facilitates communication, and makes important decisions that affect the day-to-day operations of the school. Effective use of this forum has shifted the nitty-gritty decision making out of staff meetings and into a more productive forum so that staff meetings can focus on teaching and learning.

Another group, the Patwin Leadership Council (PLC), consists of five parents and five staff members. The PLC is mandated by state law to oversee the California School Improvement and Quality Review Process; at Patwin this group also solves problems, facilitates communication, and sets policy. As part of its policy-making responsibility, the council focuses on issues related to long-term school improvement. "We are pioneering ways to involve parents as key stakeholders in the school and in leadership roles," reports Zimmerman. Other parent/staff groups that work to foster school-home collaboration are the Human Relations Committee and the Parent Teachers Association.

"My primary job is to be a teacher of adults and to facilitate adults learning from each other," Zimmerman says. "I have strong beliefs in the power of reflective practice and place high value on collaboration."

The PLC sets aside funds each year for three full days of collaboration at each grade level. Teams can choose their own topics for collaboration, and Zimmerman requires a summary of proceedings. "It has been the best expenditure of dollars I've ever seen," she exclaims. "This collaboration time was sold to the parents by explaining that it results in greater teaching equity across grade levels. While parents cannot choose a teacher, they can be assured that learning opportunities are comparable from class to class."

Teachers also have time set aside on Wednesday afternoons for staff meetings, district-level curriculum development, and teacher collaboration, Zimmerman says. She believes that the extra time teachers have to talk with one another accelerates their ability to innovate. In addition to the time mentioned above, the district provides four days of staff development—two-and-a-half days for schools and one-and-a-half days for district-level priorities. "At Patwin we rarely have the sage on the stage.

85

Instead we look at student work and have conversations about what we are learning," Zimmerman explains.

Zimmerman uses faculty meetings to model her commitment to collaboration:

> I never talk at people in staff meetings. I put information in memo form and use faculty meetings for substantive conversations. For example, this week we will have a conversation on field trips. I want them to think deeply about field trips and how to get optimal learning from these experiences. I have learned there is real power in the group conversations, and that if I can create opportunities for real dialogue, a higher consciousness will start to percolate. I believe in the power of asking questions with no answer.

In 1995 Patwin began the California accountability process referred to as the Program Quality Review (PQR). Along with long-term goal setting, the process encourages schools to study one curricular area in depth over time. Consequently, the staff decided to devote three full staff meetings to the assessment of written language, Zimmerman recalls. A schoolwide writing sample was collected, and all teachers helped to score these samples for all grades using rubrics they had developed earlier in the year. "It was very scary for teachers to present their own students' writing samples for schoolwide scrutiny," Zimmerman says. "These studies of student work must take place in an environment of high trust. Afterwards teachers reported that this project provided the best inservice experience they had ever had!"

Patwin teachers continued to study writing in 1996. They have also examined the reading-writing connection. As part of the PQR, the teachers formed research teams to learn more about ways to engage students in print. They have collected test data, survey data, and anecdotal data about their research questions and reported the findings at the first-ever Patwin Symposium. "Because of this process we have had more time to focus on schoolwide curriculum development than I ever did at my previous school," Zimmerman notes.

Zimmerman cites cognitive coaching and ASCD's Dimensions of Learning as particularly influential in her approach to staff development:

> Through these experiences, I have been part of two different communities of practice in which we learn through practice and ongoing dia-

logue. I have discovered that it is this ongoing dialogue with other deep thinkers about real issues that creates the best learning. This is what I want for the teachers at Patwin. I know that if they learn to do this, I will have helped create a culture in which everyone teaches and everyone learns.

## Muscogee County School District

The Muscogee County School District, located southwest of Atlanta near the Alabama-Georgia state line, has 34 elementary schools, 9 middle schools, and 7 high schools serving more than 32,000 students in prekindergarten through 12th grade. Extended learning programs include a night school for adults and nonconventional high school students, and a prekindergarten that enrolls approximately 750 students. The system also maintains two alternative schools—one for middle-school-aged students and one for high school students.

According to Elizabeth Thornton, director of staff development, the state legislature in 1995 provided a 6 percent pay raise for all teachers, with benefits to be covered by the local school systems. To fund the additional costs for benefits, the central office was restructured, with more than 46 central office positions eliminated. This restructuring shifted responsibility for the implementation of district initiatives to administrators and teachers.

District improvement efforts have focused on two goals adopted by the board of education: having the district exceed state and national standards in academic achievement; and promoting inclusion, trust, empowerment, and enablement for all personnel. To those ends, Thornton recalls, the district began investing several years ago in long-term training related to the school improvement process. School teams received training in school improvement planning, facilitation skills, team building, and site-based decision making. A number of teachers were also trained as school improvement facilitators. Thornton explains how national and state resources have played a role in the district:

> When we began in 1989 the National Staff Development Council recommended that each central office person adopt a school. Central office liaisons still support communication and relationships even though because of the restructuring we've all had to work with more schools. . . . About $300,000 of staff development money is allocated directly to the

schools. We are a state pilot in combining state and federal plans for staff development into one comprehensive plan and budget. The staff development department handles the accounting, the school teams control how they want that money spent.

Each school has a management team with representation from all segments of the staff, each grade level, classified employees, administration, and, in some cases, parents, Thornton says. The team members serve on a rotating basis and select their own chair and secretary. The team meets regularly to review the school's plan, monitor progress, study issues, identify solutions to problems, assess progress in action plan implementation, and reprioritize goals and objectives.

According to Thornton, the district directs all available resources of the Muscogee County School District to assist the schools. It supports school teams by providing training for all schools in site-based management, furnishing each school with comprehensive assessment information, and monitoring the progress of each school. Schools, in turn, are responsible for using the student achievement data and other measures to identify areas for improvement and for developing a comprehensive plan for student achievement. They must also establish a five-year timeline for the implementation of the comprehensive improvement plan and for establishing benchmarks for implementation and evaluation of the plan. "Beginning in December 1996, all schools are required to report directly to the school board on the progress they are making in achieving their goals," Thornton notes. "Every school is accountable for its own improvement and will be compared against their own baseline data."

Principals serve on the school management teams, but every member of the team has equal power. "What's most exciting is that schools have moved from emphasizing morale building [and] structural improvements to finally focusing on improving student achievement," Thornton observes. "It has taken some time for the schools to come around to this focus, but they are finally there."

In 1995 the staff development department organized a meeting with leaders from Columbus College. Included were the dean of education; department heads in math, science, and history; and the director of the college's Center for Excellence in Science and Math Education. The meeting's purpose was to explain the district's commitment to the improvement of student achievement and its staff development needs. According to Thornton,

> We explained to the group that most of the staff development decisions and money [were] at the discretion of the principals and management teams, and that we needed their help in providing specific content and subject area workshops to help improve student achievement, but they would need to correspond with the schools.

As a result of the "call for help," several things have occurred, Thornton reports. The Center for Excellence in Science and Math Education held an open house and invited all management teams and science and math department chairs so that teachers could see the facilities and observe demonstrations of ways the center could be of assistance. The center offered its services to help management teams look at students' test scores in math and science and custom-build training to address specific problems. The district provided seed money to help the center plan summer workshops that schools could choose to attend. Many schools have sent groups of math and science teachers to the comprehensive training sessions. In addition to the center's work, several university departments have sponsored content workshops and seminars at the college. "The college is conscious of our goal to improve student achievement, and it is listening to the needs of the schools and planning for meet them," Thornton observes. "I am seeing much more collaboration and cooperation between our district and the college."

Thornton points out that classroom teachers assume various staff development roles in the district's school improvement effort. The chair of each school management team is a teacher responsible for facilitating the team meetings and managing the school improvement process. This teacher helps decide how funds can be used to support the school's goals and, along with the principal, must sign all budget requests for staff development. "The management team chair must see the big picture," Thornton observes. "For many it means a lot more responsibility than they ever thought they might want. They certainly learn all the dynamics of making change."

In addition to their leadership role on school management teams, teachers from each school serve on the district's Staff Development Advisory Council. Thornton calls the advisors "my hands, feet, and head at the school. They are trained in how to set up courses and facilitate decisions around staff development and act as a liaison between the schools and the central office."

The Staff Development Department maintains a teacher resource room that includes a production room and a professional library for teachers and administrators. Staff development advisors and members of the management teams use the resources constantly to investigate ways to improve their schools. Study groups have been organized to examine specific teaching strategies, and principals release teachers to do research on other topics of concern. "The teacher resource room has made educational research more accessible for teachers, and they are using it to make decisions concerning school improvement," Thornton says.

The department also uses a training-of-trainers model to facilitate districtwide implementation of Georgia's Effective Teaching Program. The department has trained teachers to serve as school-based trainers and coaches. "Even though participation is optional, more than half of the schools and 170 teachers have opted for training and begun implementation," Thornton notes. The training-of-trainers model is also used to facilitate initiatives that focus on classroom management and technology. "Every year we seek to add to our repertoire of services to the schools," Thornton says.

In addition to these services, the staff development department employs three teachers on special assignment to work with new teachers. The district provides induction services during the first three years of service to more than 180 new teachers each year. The teacher on special assignment trains mentors in every school to assist new teachers during the induction period. "Our services continue to evolve because of needs. Perhaps this is a reason for our success," Thornton concludes.

# 11

## Performance Improvement for All Who Affect Student Learning

In many school systems staff development is directed primarily at teachers because teachers are viewed as having the most important influence on student learning. In these districts principals and central office administrators may attend conferences or workshops focused on their needs, but those experiences are typically isolated events with little or no follow-up. Classified and support staff seldom receive staff development.

As school staffs strive to function as teams and as schools seek to become learning organizations, learning must be an ongoing responsibility of all school employees. Everyone who affects student learning must continually upgrade his or her skills—school board trustees, superintendents and other central office administrators, principals, teachers, the various categories of support staff (e.g., aides, secretaries, bus drivers, custodians), and parents and community members who serve on policy-making boards and planning committees.

School board trustees must possess a working understanding of the change process, be conversant with the latest theory and research regarding instruction, and have the interpersonal and group skills that allow them to function as part of a smoothly operating leadership team. In addition to these understandings and skills, superintendents must continually refine their knowledge about various critical issues that affect overall district performance. Principals and teachers not only must have the knowledge, skills, and attitudes that make for effective instruction, but also must be able to successfully function on school improvement teams and other work groups. Classified and support staff not only must continually upgrade their job skills, but must consider ways they can contribute to the mission and objectives of their schools and the school system as a whole. (In one example of this, a school bus driver thought of her bus as the students' "first classroom" of the day.) The Center on Families, Communities, Schools, and Children's Learning at Johns Hopkins University and the Citrus County School District in Florida illustrate this shift in thinking.

## Center on Families, Communities, Schools, and Children's Learning

Joyce Epstein is a champion for parent involvement in education. She is codirector of the Center on Families, Communities, Schools, and Children's Learning and codirector of the Schools, Family, and Community Partnerships Program in the Center for Research on the Education of Students Placed at Risk (CRESPAR) at Johns Hopkins University in Baltimore.

Epstein has developed a framework that specifies six types of parental involvement—parenting, communicating, volunteering, learning at home, decision making, and collaborating with the community. The framework helps educators develop more comprehensive programs of school, family, and community partnerships by helping them match the appropriate practices with their desired outcomes. Epstein explains:

> No one type of involvement is more important than another. Most school improvement plans have goals in such areas as improving achievement test scores, improving attendance, completing homework, improving behavior, and creating partnerships between families and schools. Each of these goals can be supported by different types of partnerships. The framework shows that each type leads to different, important outcomes and benefits for teachers, parents, and students.

Epstein stresses the importance of linking school, family, and community partnerships to school improvement goals. For example, if a school goal is improved math achievement, an action team for school, family, and community partnerships might focus on math interactive homework so that students know that their families are interested in their work and progress in math.

"Our work with school action teams to create school, family, and community partnerships is designed to help educators see that working with parents is part of their professional responsibilities," Epstein says. Her approach to staff development helps all teachers develop capacities and expertise to communicate with families on a regular basis:

> In our work with schools the action team approach restructures staff development to enable educators and parents to work together to develop, implement, evaluate, and continuously improve the practice of partnership. This is not a "dose of inservice education." Rather it is an active form of developing staff talents, capacities, and expertise. The teachers, administrators, parents, and others on the action team for school, family, and community partnerships become the experts on this topic for their school.

The Teachers Involve Parents in Schoolwork (TIPS) interactive homework process is an example of a new form of staff development, according to Epstein. In this project teachers worked with researchers to create interactive homework that they and other teachers can use to enable students to talk with their families about what they are learning in school.

Epstein contends that districts and schools spend too many staff development dollars on outside experts, money that would be better invested in teachers in the district working with one another. She recalls how the TIPS project developed:

> With the TIPS project, each summer we paid a few teachers to work together and with us to create interactive homework activities that matched their science, language arts, and math curricula. The support went a long way because now the prototype assignments are disseminated nationally. Initially, teachers were not confident about their abilities to design interactive homework. By working with each other, editing each other's activities, testing the homework assignments, and sharing them with other teachers, they learned a new approach. This kind of investment is at least as important as bringing in outside experts. There has to be balance and redistribution of resources for staff development.

Epstein has established a new staff development initiative, the National Network of Partnership 2000 Schools, to help schools, districts, and state leaders implement and maintain effective programs of school, family, and community partnerships. Partnership 2000 schools will receive the center's assistance for the next few years to implement the six types of parental involvement. "We invite all elementary, middle, and high schools that are ready to develop better partnerships to become members of this network," she says.

## Citrus County School District

The Citrus County School District in west-central Florida serves 13,000 students in 18 schools. Retirees make up a large segment of the community, and the student population is very diverse. Barbara Spanos is a parent facilitator in a full-service school, the Lecanto Family Action Center, where several social service agencies provide support on site to students and their families. She is also a former staff development office secretary and past chair of the district's Support Staff Development Council. Each school and department chooses its representative to the council, so the council is composed of individuals with diverse roles (e.g., teacher aide, custodian).

Spanos recalls the origins of the council: "We worked with a facilitator who helped us come up with a vision and then a mission. We started with team building. It was a long process but worth it." As a result of its work, the council developed a vision and mission:

> Our vision for the future of the Citrus County support staff is that by the year 2000 we will attain total participation and commitment to professional performance. The mission of the Support Staff Development Council is to enhance support staff services for the Citrus County School System by providing a voice and creating opportunities for professional growth.

Spanos reports that the council also has five goals: (1) to improve communication and build professional image of the support staff, (2) to promote professional growth and commitment of council members, (3) to promote positive professional growth of all support staff, (4) to develop and assist with delivery of educational programs for all support staff, and (5) to promote administrative awareness and support. Various objectives and activities flow from these goals. "The committee has a lot of active members, and there are always some we wish could be more involved," Spanos notes. "We are always trying to find ways to involve and motivate others."

Some of the activities included in the support staff development plan are a new employee orientation, employee newsletters, an annual retreat for planning, full- and half-day inservice sessions, collaboration with the professional staff development program, a support staff mini-convention, and an administrators' luncheon. "We work hard to give ownership for our plans," Spanos says. "We encourage the involvement of everyone in the decision-making process at their job sites, and we try and demonstrate the connection between the support staff and the students we serve. We tell our cafeteria workers, for instance, if they aren't there the kids don't eat. Everyone has a contribution to make."

After the sudden death in 1995 of John Headlee, the director of staff development and media services, the district reorganized the staff development office, and Nancy S. Price was named as coordinator. Barbara Spanos then moved to the Lecanto Family Action Center, where she uses her staff development coordination talents to manage staff development training and consultation rooms for a variety of clients and students.

In the meantime, according to Price, the Support Staff Development Council will continue to assist the school district as it faces the challenges of continued growth and the desire to maintain the feeling of community that the district has had in the past. "The Support Staff Development Council is a very positive and powerful presence as the district undergoes change," Price says. "Barbara Spanos and others like her are key factors in the council's success, which ultimately affects all our students."

# 12

## Staff Development at the Center of Reform

Professional development of school employees and significant changes in the organizations in which they work are both required if schools are to adequately prepare students for life in a world that is becoming increasingly complex. Staff development is at the center of all education reform strategies—without it, such strategies are merely good ideas that cannot find expression.

In the past, staff development has too often been an afterthought as school systems initiated major innovations. Fortunately, more districts today are recognizing that they cannot educate all youngsters to high levels without well-designed staff development initiatives. The Forest Grove School District in Oregon provides an example of such a district.

### Forest Grove School District

Forest Grove, Oregon, is a rural community 26 miles west of Portland. The Forest Grove School District serves 4,600 students and employs 225 teachers in six elementary schools, two junior high schools, and a high school. In 1990, Superintendent Irv Nikolai brought to the district the Outcome-Driven Development Model (ODDM) from Johnson City, New York. Rosie O'Brien Vojtek, who served as a principal in the district from

1993 to 1995 and is currently the director of instruction for the Oregon City Public Schools, provides a school-based perspective on this change initiative.

The Forest Grove student population is similar to that found in many suburbs of large metropolitan areas. It includes both high-income neighborhoods and those with low-income residents and high mobility due to a large number of migrant workers. Vojtek's former school, Joseph Gale Elementary School, is located in "inner-city" Forest Grove and is the district's Chapter 1 school. Approximately 40 percent of Joseph Gale's students are Hispanic, with more than 60 percent on free and reduced lunch.

System-level consensus for ODDM was achieved before Vojtek's tenure in the district through the development of a district mission statement and beliefs, and outcomes for measuring student success. Vojtek's describes how the model has affected her work:

> The part of the process that I was taught and use the most is the four points of the success diamond the district employed to determine if what we were doing was getting us what we wanted. We ask ourselves: What do we know? What do we believe? What do we want? and What do we do to make it happen? We continuously ask ourselves if what we are doing is getting us what we wanted. If it is not, we ask, Why not? We just keep moving around the diamond to ensure what we are doing is getting us what we want.

In 1991, after the initiation of ODDM in Forest Grove, the Oregon legislature passed HB3565, referred to as the 21st Century Schools Act. Consistent with the philosophy of ODDM, it mandated content standards and outcomes to be assessed in order for students to qualify for a Certificate of Initial Mastery at approximately the 10th grade. Vojtek recalls that the Forest Grove School District used staff development to implement the kinds of curricular changes necessary to align district curriculum with state requirements:

> The expectations by the state were not unlike the previous expectations set forth in the district plan, and so it was easy to merge the two processes into one. Yet the demands on teachers were enormous as they learned new assessment procedures and made curricular changes to strengthen alignment. They were tired and sometimes frustrated, but it was our challenge to find ways to help them stay the course.

To assist schools in meeting state and district expectations, the district applied for a state-funded 21st Century Grant. Joseph Gale Elementary School received a grant for $6,000 to address the issues of family involvement and social service partnerships. Vojtek tells of how the school's site council, made up of parents, teachers, and classified members, "recognized a need to help connect families to social services and help teachers learn more about what social services are available." As a result of the grant the teachers on the site council put together a "yellow pages" resource book for teachers, parents, and other community members listing social services and how to contact them.

Another school goal, Vojtek notes, was to increase family involvement in the school. To get parents into the school, the site council and other staff members at the school cooked and served a free hot dog dinner to everyone who attended Back to School Night. The team also invited social services agencies to meet with families during the evening. "The school served meals to more than 500 people," she says, "which was a considerable increase in attendance from the previous years." The success of the kick-off event resulted in increased parental involvement throughout the year. Because translators were available to help with communication, Spanish-speaking families, especially the parents, felt more welcome.

In addition, the site council used the grant to design and offer "colearning" Spanish-English classes for both English speakers who wanted to learn Spanish and Spanish speakers who wanted to learn English. The site council also worked with the Boys and Girls Club to coordinate a summer and after-school program and with Marriott's Food Service to provide free summer breakfasts and lunches to anyone under 18. In addition, it used other monies to provide translators for all school functions and to produce its newsletter and other written communication in both English and Spanish.

Joseph Gale's site council, like other site councils in the system, was given a one-time allocation of $6,000 for staff development and school improvement planning. According to Vojtek, the first success associated with staff development was the implementation of a schoolwide discipline plan. Before the plan's implementation, Vojtek recalls, the principal's office was like a revolving door for many students. Some teachers had the philosophy that students who were not interested in learning should be removed from the classroom. Vojtek asked the site council to review the discipline policy because of the inordinate amount of time she was spending on discipline. Site council members collected data that supported her assertion, and they acknowledged that the number of students being sent to the principal's office was preventing her from being able to address many other school priorities. "It took a lot of time and discussion to get to a point where teachers acknowledged there was truly a problem," Vojtek says. Finally, the staff was ready to dedicate staff development days to working with a consultant to help write a plan and to provide training to assist with its implementation. Vojtek and many of the teachers attended summer classes as a team, and follow-up sessions were conducted throughout the following year. "That staff development effort dramatically changed the behavior and climate of the school," Vojtek says.

At that point, attention shifted to academic performance with an initial focus on the language arts. The school developed schoolwide goals and action plans, as well as grade-level action plans. As a result, test scores for the 1994–1995 statewide reading and writing assessment showed a dramatic increase in the percentage of Joseph Gale students who scored in the proficient and advanced levels. "When everyone pulls together," Vojtek points out, "when a single focus is established, when time is provided to teachers to work together, we see changes that improve what we do and how we work for students. Essential to our success has been the collaborative leadership of the site council to work with the staff and provide ownership and focus for our schoolwide improvement areas." Other contributing factors included establishing an awareness of the need for attention to language arts skills through data collection and analysis and providing staff development opportunities with adequate follow-up and support from both district and building administrators.

Another role of the site council at Joseph Gale was to decide how staff development resources could be used to help teachers participate in workshops and courses. According to the district's contract with Forest Grove teachers, tuition reimbursement must be approved by the site council based upon council-established criteria. The criteria include the alignment of course content with building goals and the contribution of the course to certification or advanced degree requirements.

The Forest Grove School District builds the knowledge and skills of school leaders by providing institutes and other training opportunities for teams of teachers who are seeking to create change in their buildings. The district also offers training for site council leadership. Individuals, grade-level teams, and site councils may ask the district for staff development assistance during the six days during the school year established by the district for this purpose.

As a principal in Forest Grove, Vojtek viewed herself as a teacher of teachers:

> I served as a facilitator, consultant, instructor, and colleague who assisted teachers in integrating curriculum, using new instructional strategies, and improving the quality of life of all students in their classrooms. I promoted different forms of staff development, but the most important thing I did was "walk the talk." I facilitated learning through inquiry—asking tough questions; managing the change process; serving as a cheerleader, supporter, and advocate for teachers; keeping the vision out front; acting as a buffer to the central office as well as a communication link; and helping to connect people to different support services and resources. To do this, it is critical to get to know teachers on an individual basis, to know their needs, and to help them celebrate their successes. As a principal, it was important that I knew when to push a little harder and when to help them pull back because they were taking on too much. Staff development is the most important thing we can offer teachers or anyone. The day we stop learning is the day we become a dead society. There is so much out there to learn and assimilate. All staff members—both certified and classified—need to continue to read, to question, to talk with one another, and to expand on the knowledge they have. We owe it to our students.

# References

Brooks, J., and M. Brooks. (1993). *The Case for Constructivist Classrooms*. Alexandria, Va.: ASCD.

Calhoun, E.F. (1994). *How to Use Action Research in the Self-Renewing School*. Alexandria, Va.: ASCD.

Clinchy, B.M. (1995). "Goals 2000: The Student as Object." *Phi Delta Kappan 76*, 5: 383, 389–392.

Darling-Hammond, L., and M. McLaughlin. (1995). "Policies That Support Professional Development in an Era of Reform." *Phi Delta Kappan 76*, 8: 597–604.

Deming, W.E. (1986). *Out of the Crisis*. Cambridge, Mass.: Massachusetts Institute of Technology.

Fitzpatrick, K. (1995). "An Outcomes-Based Systems Perspective on Establishing Curricular Coherence." In *Toward a Coherent Curriculum*, edited by J.A. Beane. Alexandria, Va.: ASCD.

Fritz, R. (1989). *The Path of Least Resistance*. New York: Fawcett Columbine.

Fullan, M. (1991). *The New Meaning of Educational Change*. New York: Teachers College Press.

Guskey, T. (1990). "Integrating Innovations." *Educational Leadership 47*, 5: 17-24.

Holzman, M. (1993). "What Is Systemic Change?" *Educational Leadership 51*, 1: 18.

Lieberman, A. (1995). "Practices That Support Teacher Development." *Phi Delta Kappan 76*, 8: 591–596.

O'Neil, J. (1993). "Turning the System on Its Head." *Educational Leadership 51*, 1: 8–13.

O'Neil, J. (1994). "Aiming for New Outcomes: The Promise and the Reality." *Educational Leadership 51*, 6: 6–10.

Sarason, S. (1991). *The Predictable Failure of Educational Reform*. San Francisco: Jossey-Bass.

Senge, P. (1990). *The Fifth Discipline: The Art and Discipline of the Learning Organization*. New York: Doubleday.

Shulman, L. (1986). "Those Who Understand: Knowledge Growth in Teaching." *Educational Researcher 15*, 2: 4–14.

Sparks, D., and S. Loucks-Horsley. (1989). "Five Models of Teacher Development." *Journal of Staff Development 10*, 4: 40–57.

**Dianne Aucamp**
Broward County Public Schools
Director of Human Resource Department
600 SE Third Avenue
Ft. Lauderdale, FL 33301
  Phone: 305-765-6335
  Fax:  305-760-7353
  E-mail: None

**Kathryn Blumsack**
Coordinator/Director of School Improvement Training Unit
Montgomery County Schools
850 Hungerford Drive, Room 241
Rockville, MD 20850
  Phone: 301-279-3444
  Fax:  301-279-3452
  E-mail: KBlumsack@aol.com

**Martin Brooks**
Superintendent of Schools
Valley Stream USD #13
585 N. Corona Avenue
Valley Stream, NY 11580
  Phone: 516-568-6100
  Fax:  516-568-6115
  E-mail: MGBROOKS12@aol.com

**Cathy Caro-Bruce**
Staff and Organization Development Specialist
Madison Metropolitan School District
545 West Dayton Street
Madison, WI 53711
  Phone: 608-266-6456
  Fax:  608-267-1635
  E-mail: ccarobru@facstaff.wisc.edu

**Sandee Crowther**
Division Director of Evaluation and Standards
Lawrence Public Schools
3705 Clinton Parkway
Lawrence, KS 66047
  Phone: 913-832-5000
  Fax:  913-832-5016
  E-mail: SandeeCrow@aol.com

**Rick DuFour**
Superintendent
Stevenson High School District #125
Two Stevenson Drive
Lincolnshire, IL 60069
       Phone:   847-634-4000, ext. 268
       Fax:     847-634-0239
       E-mail:  rdufour@district125.k12.il.us

**Joyce Epstein**
Codirector/Principal Research Scientist
Center on School, Family, and Community Partnerships
The Johns Hopkins University
3506 North Charles Street
Baltimore, MD 21216
       Phone:   410-516-8807
       Fax:     410-516-8890
       E-mail:  jestein@scov.csos.jhu.edu

**Jacquie Estee**
Director of Staff Development
Westside Community Schools
909 S. 76th Street
Omaha, NE 68114
       Phone:   402-390-2123
       Fax:     402-390-2136
       E-mail:  jacquie_estee@internet.esu3.k-12.ne.us

**Joe Frattaroli**
Chief Operating Officer
Teachers Academy for Math and Science
3424 State Street
Chicago, IL 60616
       Phone:   312-949-2422
       Fax:     312-808-9257
       E-mail:  None

**Howard Hardin**
Director of Clark Projects
Jefferson County Public Schools
VanHoose Education Center
P.O. Box 34020
Louisville, KY 40232-4020
       Phone:   502-485-3551
       Fax:     502-485-3821
       E-mail:  hhardin/@vhc2.jefferson.k12.ky.us

**Kathryn Harwell**
Assistant Superintendent of Instructional Services
Grapevine-Colleyville ISD
3051 Ira E. Woods Avenue
Grapevine, TX 76051-3897
      Phone:   817-488-9588, ext. 379
      Fax:      817-424-3271
      E-mail:  kharwell@tenet.edu

**Linda Hawkins**
Principal/Cognitive Coaching Consultant
Carrolton-Farmers Branch ISD
100 Swisher Road (home)
Shady Shores, TX 76207
      Phone:   214-323-6612 (office)
      Fax:      817-321-5484 (home)
      E-mail:  None

**Michael Hibbard**
Assistant Superintendent
Regional School District #15
286 Whittemore Road
Middlebury, CT 06762
      Phone:   203-758-8250
      Fax:      203-758-1908
      E-mail:  None

**Stephanie Hirsh**
Associate Executive Director
National Staff Development Council
7602 Kilmichael Lane
Dallas, TX 75248
      Phone:   972-661-2924
      Fax:      972-934-2924
      E-mail:  nsdchirsh@aol.com

**Mary Hopper**
Instructional Team Leader
San Diego City Schools
1775 Chatsworth Boulevard, Room 100
San Diego, CA 92107
      Phone:   619-225-3478
      Fax:      619-223-3947
      E-mail:  None

**Joellen Killion**
Staff Development Specialist
Adams Twelve Five Star Schools
Staff Development Training
11080 Grant Drive
Northglenn, CO 80233-3312
> Phone: 303-452-3002
> Fax: 303-450-3777
> E-mail: KILLIONJ@aol.com

**Judy Mumme**
Program Director
Mathematics Renaissance Program
570 Airport Way
Camarillo, CA 93010-8500
> Phone: 805-388-4415
> Fax: 805-388-4427
> E-mail: mumme@cams.edu

**Linda O'Neal**
Director of Staff Development
Northeast ISD
8961 Tesoro Drive
San Antonio, TX 78217
> Phone: 210-804-7192
> Fax: 210-804-7194
> E-mail: loneal@tenet.edu

**Nancy S. Price**
Coordinator of Staff Development
Citrus County School District
1007 West Main Street
Inverness, FL 34450
> Phone: 904-726-1931
> Fax: 904-726-0404
> E-mail: None

**Carole Schmidt**
Director of Professional Development
Tucson USD
1010 E. Tenth Street
Tucson, AZ 85719
> Phone: 520-617-7206
> Fax: 520-617-7381
> E-mail: katswin@aol.com

**Kay Shaw**
Director of Staff Development
Aurora Public Schools
1085 Peoria Street
Aurora, CO 80011
>    Phone:  303-344-8060, ext. 370
>    Fax:    303-340-0863
>    E-mail:  None

**Pam Smith**
Richardson Independent School District
Director of Instructional Management Effectiveness Training
400 S. Greenville
Richardson, TX 75081
>    Phone:  214-301-3372
>    Fax:    214-301-3390
>    E-mail:  pam.smith@richardson.k12.tx.us

**Barbara Spanos**
Parent Facilitator
Citrus County School Board
2575 S. Panther Pride Drive
Lecanto, FL 34461
>    Phone:  352-527-0090
>    Fax:    352-527-1410
>    E-mail:  None

**Dennis Sparks**
Executive Director
National Staff Development Council
1124 West Liberty Street
Ann Arbor, MI 48103
>    Phone:  313-998-0574
>    Fax:    313-998-0628
>    E-mail:  sparksnsdc@aol.com

**Elizabeth Thornton**
Director of Staff Development
Muscogee County School District
P.O. Box 2427
Columbus, GA 31902
>    Phone:  706-649-0608
>    Fax:    706-649-1906
>    E-mail:  ethornto@cbus.mindspring.com

**Mariam True**
Specialist in High Performance in Teaching and Learning
San Diego City Schools
1775 Chatsworth Boulevard, Room 114
San Diego, CA 92107
  Phone: 619-225-3500
  Fax:  619-225-1420
  E-mail: None

**Rosie O'Brien Vojtek**
Director of Instruction
Oregon City School District
P.O. Box 591
Oregon City, OR 97045
  Phone: 503-656-4283
  Fax:  503-657-2492
  E-mail: vojtekr1@mail.clackesd.k12.or.us

**Stephanie Webb**
Teacher on Assignment in Staff Development
The School District of Lee County
2055 Central Avenue
Fort Myers, FL 33901
  Phone: 941-337-8362
  Fax:  941 337-8388
  E-mail: stephaniew@lee.k12.fl.us

**Jody Westbrook**
Independent Consultant
Jody M. Westbrook and Associates
P.O. Drawer 519
LaCoste, TX 78039
  Phone: 210-985-9104
  Fax:  Same
  E-mail: jodywestbr@aol.com

**Diane Zimmerman**
Principal
Patwin Elementary School
4323 Cadenasso Lane
Suisun, CA 94585
  Phone: 916-757-5383
  Fax:  916-757-5417
  E-mail: DPZimmer@aol.com

**Dennis Sparks** is Executive Director of the National Staff Development Council. He can be reached at 1124 West Liberty St., Ann Arbor, MI 48103. Phone: 313-998-0574. Fax: 313-998-0628. E-mail: sparksnsdc@aol.com.

**Stephanie Hirsh** is Associate Executive Director of the National Staff Development Council. She can be reached at 7602 Kilmichael Lane, Dallas, TX 75248. Phone: 214-661-2924. Fax: 214-934-2924. E-mail: nsdchirsh@aol.com.

The National Staff Development Council (NSDC) is a nonprofit educational association with 8,000 members. The Council is committed to ensuring high levels of learning and performance for all students and staff members. NSDC regards high quality staff development as essential in creating schools in which all students and staff members are successful. The Council publishes *The Journal of Staff Development*, *The Developer*, and *The School Team Innovator*. Information about membership, the Council's annual conference, or NSDC products and services can be obtained by contacting the NSDC Business Office: P.O. Box 240, Oxford, OH 45056. Phone: 513-523-6029. Fax: 513-523-0638. E-mail: nsdchavens@aol.com.